The
Real
Steele:

The
Unauthorized
Biography
of Dakota
Johnson

New York Times
Best-selling Author

Marc Shapiro

For more information contact:
Riverdale Avenue Books
5676 Riverdale Avenue
Riverdale, NY 10471.

www.riverdaleavebooks.com

Design by www.formatting4U.com
Cover by Scott Carpenter

Digital ISBN 9781626011540
Print ISBN 9781626011557

First Edition February 2015

THIS BOOK IS DEDICATED TO...

As always my wife Nancy, my first, last and always. My daughter Rachael. My granddaughter Lily. Brent, Robert and Layla, the new additions to my universe. My agent Lori Perkins who always gets it right. Mike, Brady and Mr. Fitch, the old hands and feet. Those who create good literature, good art and good music and who are dedicated to leaving their mark. And finally to Dakota Johnson, a living, breathing example that talent will out.

TABLE OF CONTENTS

AUTHOR'S NOTES
LONGHAND BECOMES YOU

I've been asked two questions pretty consistently since I undertook the task of writing a biography on Dakota Johnson. The first is who is Dakota Johnson? A fair question. If we're all being honest here, nobody really knew who the hell she was. Yours truly included. First question answered.

Which invariably leads into…

How can you write a book-length manuscript about somebody whose entire life and career can be summed up in three paragraphs on Wikipedia? That, to this author, remains the more pertinent bone to be picked at.

But there is a precedent for there being a Dakota Johnson on the brink of stardom. Hollywood has a tradition of being built on a foundation of starlets coming in off the street literal unknowns and achieving stardom. Do the names Lana Turner and Lauren Bacall ring a bell?

But Dakota's rise is, by Tinsel Town standards, a road that jogs to the right rather than the left. *Fifty Shades of Grey* is considered an important picture, a blockbuster of massive proportions in the making. A lot is riding on it. Careers. Jobs. Perceptions. With all too rare exceptions, handing off the leading role to somebody with little or no history has been considered risky at best and foolhardy at worst.

You get the picture. A lot of people could be walking the plank because of Dakota. Including Dakota. Digression over. Now back to business.

Dakota Johnson did not arrive on the brink of stardom in the role of Anastasia Steele in the upcoming *Fifty Shades of Grey* movie a complete blank slate. But let's be honest here, this offspring of uber actors Don Johnson and Melanie Griffith has had little more than a slight career at best.

In general, Hollywood is littered with the figurative corpses of the children of celebrities who tried unsuccessfully to follow in their parent's footsteps. The rare success of a Jolie or a Fonda is more than balanced out by the failed acting careers of people whose last names of their parents were synonymous with superstardom. That's just the way it goes in Hollywood.

A long-form article would have most certainly sufficed for Dakota Johnson in most worlds. There are self-publishers all over the internet who can be relied on to be first out of the box with a 2500 word magazine article masquerading as an e book in an attempt to catch the first wave of celebrity mania. A perfect example of this sort of business being the quickie Lorde' book that clocks in at a massive 11 pages. But that does not work in the world of big time, big publishing celebrity biographies. The people who live and die by these books like a little meat on the bones.

So what's a writer to do with a subject whose life and times are no bigger than the length of a fingernail?

Well for openers there is the tried and true...research. First and foremost track down everybody who knew Dakota Johnson personally and professionally and get them to talk about her. I found a couple who were willing to talk and can guarantee what they told me was insightful. Second, and of equal importance, track down everything that has ever been written about her. And in the case of Dakota Johnson, much of that, like their subject, is a bit on the skimpy side. What to do? What to do?

In the case of Dakota Johnson there would be no shorthand.

As most pop columnists and bloggers go, shorthand is the preferred tool. If one line can tell the story, use one line. If you've written more than 500 words, then you've probably overwritten in a world populated by short attention spans and *USA Today*. But in writing about Dakota Johnson, I've turned the tables and dug deep for every element, quote and anecdote and layered on all the information I could find on the moment in Dakota Johnson's life.

What was she feeling when she slept with Justin Timberlake's character in *The Social Network*? How pertinent was that moment to the film? What was it like on the set that day? Did her boyfriend object? You get the picture. This is not merely a Post-It note. This is lines, paragraphs and, yes, most importantly, pages. An archaeological expedition into the moments and minutiae that make up the life of Dakota Jackson.

Her stint in rehab? If it were not for *The National Enquirer*, that bastion of topflight investigative journalism (and I'm not being totally flip here), nobody would have had a clue that Dakota Johnson had a drinking and drug problem. And because it was Dakota Johnson, the story essentially died from lack of interest.

Another puzzle to be pieced together. Her current, at the moment, boyfriend being a Scientologist? The movie she did that does not appear on her filmography and, most likely, was never released? Both blaring headlines that deserve more than a cursory look.

For somebody who few actually knew, Dakota Johnson's story banked a whole lot of mental sweat equity. And an eye on the news which diligently chronicled her rise to celebrity-in-the-making.

Those late to the dance probably recognize Dakota as the co-star of the much-anticipated *Fifty Shades of Grey*, the compelling love story that happens to take in handcuffs, whips and all manner of sadomasochism. But Dakota did not get to this point by accident. There was that little snippet of a scene in *The Social Network* that set Hollywood hearts a flutter. Dakota had been more than the sexy cipher. In a shade under three minutes, she had created sufficient backstory and character to elevate what even her director had admitted was a thankless role and made it shine.

She was very good in some mainstream entertainment like *21 Jump Street, The Five Year Engagement* and *Need For Speed* as well as the likes of small independent outings like *Gay Dude* and *Chloe and Theo* which you might have missed. But bottom line, Dakota has put in her time. As did this writer in pulling it all together.

Hard work? You bet it was. But it is hard work born of a desire to paint as complete a picture as possible of a total unknown whose name, a year from now, will be on everybody's lips. You heard it here first.

Marc Shapiro 2015

INTRODUCTION
IF THIS BE ANASTASIA

The final decision had millions of *Fifty Shades of Grey* fans in the proverbial dither from the moment it had been announced that the world wide literary sensation *Fifty Shades of Grey* would make the not unexpected translation to the big screen.

How literal a translation of the book would the movie be? Would the film be a more conventional R rated outing or would a thinking out of the box director literally let it all hang out? Where would it be shot? When would it be released? Once the mundane questions were out of the way, the one question on everybody's mind would eventually leap to the fore.

Who would play Anastasia Steele?

This would not be the typical big budget studio film casting announcement. This would be a movie, and hopefully movies, whose books had already impacted millions of reader's lives. E.L. James had struck a highly charged, emotional chord in millions of readers around the world. And as usually happens, Hollywood immediately smelled money in the water and rushed in to cash in.

Much like *Twilight* and *Harry Potter*, there was a

sense of propriety and personal and emotional investment coursing through every fiber of the issue. The producers, directors and studios would ultimately have the final say. Reportedly author EL James had a clause e in her contract that would allow for her involvement in any casting issues. But they all knew that there was a sense of volatility and expectation in *Fifty Shades* fandom that could quickly turn on them if they were not careful.

The fans wanted it their way.

Consequently the ink had barely dried on the press release when the followers of *Fifty Shades* were bombarding the Internet with fevered suggestions of who they thought should play the very kinky star-crossed lovers. Particular attention was focused on who should play the role of Anastasia Steele, the submissive but ultimately spunky and defiant counter to the sexually and obsessively twisted Christian Grey. In their minds, they had lived and breathed the books. So obviously they knew better than any producer or executive in Hollywood.

Not surprisingly, most of the suggestions, nay demands, that fired out of fandom were familiar favorites, many already star status name brands, tossed into the blogosphere with little more than a 'This is who should play Anastasia!" without an acknowledgement that putting *Fifty Shades of Grey* on the big screen and being true to the source material would not be as easy as putting 'the flavor of the moment' in front of the camera, being naked and having S&M sex.

Consequently, the list of those whose names had been batted about as the person who 'must play

Anastasia' ran the gamut of interest and notoriety. There were many mid-level actresses who saw *Fifty Shades* as a career-maker who readily acknowledged their willingness to take on the role and take off their clothes. Many more established women, leery of their careers being sidetracked by the film, said they were not interested when questioned by the media. There were valid points to be made from all corners.

For openers, the very blatant, twisted and out there nature of the film's overriding sexuality would be a put off to any established starlet who would think twice about jeopardizing their status in Hollywood by baring all. And at any level, it would take an actress of some depth to carry off Anastasia both as a flesh and blood character and in the sex scenes. The stigma of pornography being populated by bad actresses who were on board only because of their looks and their willingness to do the deed was definitely on the minds of the *Fifty Shades of Grey* producers. Most fan suggestions were readily acknowledged, as were the blatant publicity ploys of unknowns who saw a blog headline in just saying they were or were not interested in the role.

And although it was rarely spoken, behind the scenes of casting Anastasia was the lasting memory of a movie with a similar vibe and what its failure had done to the actress playing the lead. The movie *Showgirls* was, similarly, hyped to near exhaustion and as had been the casting of Elizabeth Berkeley in the lead role. Bottom line, *Showgirls* was the worst kind of bomb, the kind always laughed at and, to this day, is still high on the list of the worst movies ever made. It came as no surprise that Berkeley's career never recovered. The fact that *Fifty Shades of Grey* seemingly had the same potential for disaster immediately sent many actresses running in the opposite direction.

Fifty Shades of Grey was being talked up as erotica and art rather than smut and to make that a reality was going to require thinking way outside the expected templates of Hollywood. This was very much in evidence when the producers announced two women in the key creative roles, director Sam Taylor Johnson and screenwriter Kelly Marcel.

Credits for both were sparse but truly eclectic. Johnson was known primarily for the well-reviewed feature *Nowhere Boy* and a series of respected shorts. The director also made headlines on a personal front when she began a much-publicized relationship with a much younger actor from **Nowhere Boy** that ended in a thus far successful marriage. Screenwriter Marcel, likewise, had limited credits; writer for the film *Mr. Banks*, creator of the short-lived television series *Terra Nova* and, in her theater days, she conceived and mounted the UK version of *Debbie Does Dallas: The Musical*.

Both were considered deep and creative thinkers, albeit with razor-sharp commercial instincts, who immediately saw *Fifty Shades of Grey* as more art than exploitation. Coming from a woman's perspective, *Fifty Shades of Grey* could not help but be good or, at the very least, interesting.

How the casting process was progressing was a fairly well-kept secret but, as reported by Mail Online shortly after the announcement of the actors who would play the title roles, Charlie Hunnam, who, according to reports, had already clinched the role of Christian, had stealth auditions with a number of young actresses in a hotel room under the watchful eyes of the director, reportedly getting into character by talking, touching and squeezing each other.

While the names of those in the auditions were kept under wraps, there was an indication that those potential Anastasias who came across as too submissive in the more intimate moments of the audition were quickly eliminated. But also, according to reports after the fact, there was one actress who had pretty much nailed the part in a highly believable and, yes, hot audition.

A further hint as to which direction *Fifty Shades* was going came on September 2, 2013 with the announcement by *Fifty Shades of Grey* author E.L. James that actress Dakota Johnson had been selected to portray Anastasia Steele. The reaction from the public was immediate. Everybody wanted to know…

Who was Dakota Johnson?

Dakota was an actress and model who had been flying largely below the radar for quite some time. Lavish modeling spreads that made her the darling of the fashion world. Small parts in big films and big parts in small films made Dakota, at that point, a novelty whose lineage, the daughter of actors Don Johnson and Melanie Griffith, seemed the main point of intrigue. To that point, Dakota had gone with the flow. The sporadic interviews she had done seemed almost matter of fact. She had talked pretty much about the obvious elements of her life in a fairly laidback, almost flower child manner. Nothing in her career had seemingly been that important.

Until the call went out for an actress to play Anastasia Steele.

At which point, Dakota was, as the world would come to realize, suddenly and unexpectedly, obsessed.

Dakota was at an emotional and professional crossroads. She was doing good works in films that, largely, went unnoticed. In her own mind, she was not certain if she was ready to carry a film like *Fifty Shades* or if she ever would be. For Dakota, it was angst coupled with the fact that a movie like *Fifty Shades* could make or irrevocably break her career. But deep down in the place where art and emotion dwell, she knew she had to go for it.

Quite uncharacteristically, Dakota pleaded with her manager to get her a shot at the part. It would have been a daring move for her reps to put somebody who was a novice up for such an important role. But there had always been an earnestness and determination in Dakota that they had quietly admired and so, while secretly they must have felt she was an extreme longshot at best, they figured the audition experience could not hurt and so they said okay.

In the meantime, Dakota took her preparation for the role very seriously. She read all three volumes of the *Fifty Shades* odyssey and was quick to find the style and substance to what many high-minded critics had deemed trash.

Given Dakota's attitude toward life and art, it did not come as a surprise that the actress saw highbrow potential in something most dismissed as throwaway lowbrow. Dakota saw character where others simply saw blatant sex and cardboard characters. The actress felt she could make this work and she was prepared to take on all comers when it came to getting the role.

Likewise, the actress walked into the audition

well-armed with what she felt would be the perfect performance piece, a long sexually explicit passage from the classic Ingmar Bergman film *Persona*. The producers and director were impressed with her reading. They liked her look. Dakota left the audition knowing she had done her best. Now it was just a matter of waiting for the call that may or may not come.

One thing was certain. As controversial as *Fifty Shades of Grey* was, with many predicting either career-making or career-ending for whoever landed the coveted roles, actresses known, marginally known and totally unknown, were lining up to take their shot at Anastasia Steele. The audition process was arduous and mentally exhausting. Many fell out because they could not handle the psychological underpinnings of the role. Some quite simply changed their minds. As the auditions continued, the number of actresses still in the running were reportedly trimmed down to a select handful that included the likes of Alicia Vikander, Imogen Potts, Elizabeth Olsen, Shailene Woodley, Felicity Jones and the dark horse candidacy of Kristen Stewart. The latter of which received an official vote of no confidence when *Fifty Shades* author E.L. James said an emphatic no to the idea of an actress going from *Twilight* to *Fifty Shades*. To the surprise of many, Dakota was still on the list.

And having made it this far, the pressure was starting to get to her.

In the ensuing days, Dakota was constantly on the phone with her manager and agent, begging for even the slightest bit of information regarding how the casting was going. For Dakota, this was new and unchartered territory. In a short career, she had become used to the vague and unpredictable nature of Hollywood and, by association, took each victory and disappointment in stride. But *Fifty Shades* was a different animal. This was an opportunity she cared deeply about.

In the parlance of the movie biz, Dakota landed the role after several meetings with the director and producers. There were singular talkabouts in which she was questioned about her feeling about the character of Anastasia and how she felt the direction of the movie should go. Then, as reported by *The Wrap, TMZ* and countless other media outlets, the final hurdle was an on video 'chemistry read' with actor Charlie Hunnam who was everybody's favorite to portray Christian Grey. The result of that read was enthusiastically tweeted by co-producer Michael De Luca who proclaimed, "The auditions were stunning. There was incredible chemistry."

Dakota was on holiday in New York when the phone finally rang. "I remember looking out of my apartment window at all the apartments across the street," she recalled to *Entertainment Weekly*. "I thought about how funny it would be if I was watching people having sex." This image gave way to the reality that Dakota had landed the role of a lifetime.

"When they told me I had the part, I just cried and cried," she told *Entertainment Weekly*.

Once people got past the fact that she was the daughter of two celebrities of a bygone era, actors Don Johnson and Melanie Griffith, the pickings, as they were presented in the press announcements of her landing the role of Anastasia, were rather slim. Former model turned actress who had small, fairly insignificant parts in the films *The Social Network, Need For Speed* and *21 Jump Street*. The two pops of legitimate recognition came in a co-starring role in the film *The Five Year Engagement* and, most recently, in the television series *Ben and Kate* which, despite so-so ratings, had been canceled after one season. To the media observers who collectively scratched their heads at the choice, Dakota Johnson had done a whole lot of not much.

Granted, Johnson seemed to have the Anastasia 'look', a mixture of shy, sultry and seductive, eyes fluid rather than harsh and capable of a variety of emotions, the ideal type for Christian Grey's manipulative and domineering ways. To look at Dakota Johnson was to take a peek back at what was perceived as 'Old Hollywood,' a mixture of light and stylish. That she looked like a very young Meryl Streep only added to the equation. And by all reports, she was a capable actress within a limited body of work in which, according to reports, she stole every scene she was in. And those who had worked with her were lining up to sing her praises.

In a *New York Post* article, Dana Fox, creator of the short-lived television series, *Ben and Kate*, offered that, "She used to do physical stuff for us like Lucille Ball. She had that thing and so we used it. She was always like 'I'll do whatever it takes to make this funny.' "

The same *Post* article offered up praise from director and screenwriter Daniel Barnz whose film *Beastly* featured Dakota. "She has this combination of natural intelligence and this sort of appealing unconscious sexuality. I think there's something unpredictable about her on screen. She makes her characters really come alive."

The drawback? To the world at large she was largely a faceless, obscure non entity. *Fifty Shades* had already cost a studio and production company a lot of upfront money. The pressure on everyone connected to the movie franchise was already immense and would continue to be so. Dakota was still very much wet behind the ears. Would she be able to handle the worldwide scrutiny that would most certainly come?

And as the *Fifty Shades'* producers would discover over the next few days, she was light years away from being the people's choice for Anastasia. Not surprisingly, fan bases could be a double-edged sword. We've seen it with *Harry Potter, Twilight* and, most recently, the announcement of Ben Affleck as the next Batman. Die-hard fans fall in love with a pop culture character and can become very possessive. They feel they own it and, with a blind eye to the reality and bottom line of show business, feel they can dictate the terms in which their favorite is portrayed.

Consequently the fan base of *50 Shades* was about to declare war.

Within a matter of days a fan group had out an petition up on **Change.org** which had collected nearly 50,000 signatures, demanding that former *Gilmore Girls* TV series actress Alexis Bledel be cast in the film. There were also the not-too-veiled nasty Internet put-downs of Dakota as somebody who was, in no particular order, too fat, too thin, too edgy, too bland and a scavenger profiting off the reputation of her celebrity parents. Although infantile and immature, these low blows were coming from the very people who would, hopefully, plunk down their money to see the film. All the hoped for positive press surrounding the announcement had been high jacked by a group of fans that had suddenly grown fangs and were demanding that Focus Features do things their way.

The public's distain for Dakota Johnson would remain front-page Internet news for several days.

Dana Brunetti, one of the film's producers, had already experienced fanaticism with the development of the *Fifty Shades* project and had been good natured and, yes, accommodating in dealing with it. But he appeared more than a bit annoyed when he tweeted a response.

"There's a lot that goes into casting that isn't just looks," he said. "Talent, availability, their desire to do it, chemistry. So if your favorite isn't cast, it is most likely due to something on that list. Keep that in mind while hating and keep perspective."

Tom Todoroff, Dakota's acting teacher from back in the day, was quite happy with the news that Dakota had landed the film. "Of course there will be opinions both ways," he told the author in 2013. "Dakota's just been cast in what the world considers the movie version of a very controversial book. Dakota did not court that controversy. She just happened upon it. But being that she grew up around celebrity, I don't think she will have any trouble handling it."

Dakota quickly became the center of a celebrity crazed public. Every little known element of her life and limited career to that point was trotted out in blaring headlines. Paparazzi suddenly became more diligent in pursuing her then the often afterthought they had considered her years previous. Her most mundane news items or public appearances went viral on the Internet all over the world. And when it was discovered that her current boyfriend, actor Jordan Masterson, was a Scientologist, the tabloids went wild in a very Katie Holmes/Tom Cruise sort of way.

This was an aspect of celebrity Dakota had never been close to. But she was fearless in the face of the media spotlight, projecting that naughty but innocent look and, according to her mother in an *OMG Insider* interview, showing no concern.

"She's not the type of person to be scared," declared Griffith. "She has never been that way. When she was two, she was not scared."

Point of fact, Dakota seemed surprisingly neutral to the sudden onslaught in the media, both good and bad. Sudden stardom on such a massive level could have wilted lesser souls but Dakota, perhaps because of her celebrity studded lineage, had seen all the trappings before. So, on the surface, she presented a quiet, yet grateful persona to that first crush of big time press.

But the young actress was also well-aware of what was to come in this unexpected turn.

Being in *Fifty Shades* would almost guarantee her sudden elevation to A-list status in Hollywood. Unless she turned out to be a critical disaster and/or the trio of projected movies became a laughing stock, her future was secured. In the swirl of all these possible scenarios she was determined to keep her life as normal as possible.

At the time of her selection, Dakota was right in the middle of another movie, *Cymbaline* and was putting all her energy into this modern re-telling of classic Shakespeare tale. In those moments around family and friends during the first *Fifty Shades* media blitz, she was simply Dakota.

"The only thing she has told me," Griffith shared with *OMG Insider*, "was to please make me do the dishes when I go home. She wants everything in her life to stay really normal."

Besides, pending an unexpected turn of events or an act of God, it was already too late. *Fifty Shades of Grey* had already been in active pre-production mode for some months and would have to begin production sometime around October if the film were to make its August, 2014 release date.

And so like it or not, little known and largely unheralded actress Dakota Johnson would be the world's Anastasia Steele.

CHAPTER ONE
MEET THE PARENTS

There were a lot of Don Johnson types in Hollywood by the early 1970's. Talented actors, like Peter Fonda and Jack Nicholson, who had come of age the previous decade, all brash, flamboyant and unconventional. Brilliant on screen and wild in their personal life, they were the new standard in a Hollywood that had evolved in the 60's and hell bent on making creative magic on the silver screen. But ultimately Don Johnson was the prototype, the blueprint of style, substance and craziness that others quite naturally followed into the 'me' decade.

By Hollywood standards, Don Johnson had already lived a lifetime by the time he began work on the film *The Harrad Experiment* in 1973.

Already married and divorced twice and coming off a much-publicized relationship with notorious rock groupie Pamela Des Barres, the then 22 year-old actor was already a grizzled veteran both personally and (on the strength of countless television appearances and a couple of low budget films) professionally. But despite a fistful of credits and glowing reviews, Johnson was still considered B level, somebody who had most certainly walked the walk but, in the eyes of decision makers in Hollywood, was not yet ready for his close up. Don was an old school pragmatist mixed in with a slightly heathen bent. Which is why he said yes to *The Harrad Experiment*.

The Harrad Experiment was just the latest stop on the Hollywood grind that would ultimately see him strike gold in the television series *Miami Vice*. But Sonny Crockett was still light years away and the bills had to be paid. And so there was *The Harrad Experiment*, a melodramatic and, by early 70's standards, sexually charged tale of post summer of love free and experimental love based on a wildly successful and controversial book of the day.

It was on the set of *The Harrad Experiment* that Johnson first laid eyes on a very cute and perky 14 year-old extra named Melanie Griffith.

Griffith, the daughter of legendary actress Tippi Hedren and Peter Griffith, had taken a rather leisurely road through Hollywood with a commercial at the ripe old age of nine months and a couple of extra roles. *The Harrad Experiment* being essentially more of the same. Just stand around, looking as hot as was legally allowed in Hollywood at the time and smiling that oh-so-enticing smile.

The attraction between Griffith and Johnson was immediate. Johnson was cautious in the face of their obvious age difference and the fact that, even in the face of a permissive Hollywood, was not of legal age. Griffith, adult and seductive beyond her years, was overtly aggressive in her flirtations with Johnson. "Melanie and I became friends first," Johnson recalled in *People*, "but then she picked me for something more."

This being Hollywood in the more liberal 70's, nobody gave it much notice that the 22 year-old Johnson and the 14 year-old Griffith became romantically involved over the course of filming on *The Harrad Experiment.* "From the first there's been nothing hidden about our relationship," Johnson told *People.*

The pair were considered the hot romance in Tinsel town for the next year, many in the scandal and gossip press predicting that it was an affair that would rapidly flame out or even worse land Johnson in some legal trouble. But the relationship endured to the point where, by the time Griffith had turned 15, she and Johnson had taken the next step of moving in together. In a rented Laurel Canyon house populated by lots of dogs, the young couple's relationship flourished. Again more tongues wagged. But Johnson and Griffith were believably in love and effectively turned a blind eye to it all.

Melanie's mother, Tippi Hedren had grudgingly given her approval of her daughter's situation. Bottom line, she was not having to pay their rent. Because professionally Melanie and Don were doing quite well on their own.

The degree in which Melanie had been willing to dance around nudity on screen (or in many cases with the aid of a body double) had jumpstarted her career in notable movies like *The Drowning Pool, Night Moves* and *Smile* while Don continued to find often revealing and lurid B movie work in the likes of *Return To Macon County.* This being the swinging 70's, it was not surprising that their liberal attitudes headed off any conflicts about Melanie appearing nude in films.

"Don doesn't own my body," Melanie said in a *People* article. For his part Don, in the same article, acknowledged that "I'm hardly in a position to object to her nudity."

In 1976 they would make things legal when they married. It was all idyllic at first but it did not take long for the dire predictions of the press to come true. Their marriage would last a mere six months, reportedly succumbing to the pressures of Hollywood and Johnson's reputation as a party guy prone to alcoholic binges and drug use. Griffith's mother, Tippi Hedren, had been less than enthusiastic about her daughter's relationship with this much older man to start with and was surprised, albeit not thrilled, when they made their relationship legal. Hedren had told *People* that she had not liked the idea of them getting married at a small church in Las Vegas. Ultimately she was thankful that the marriage had not worked out.

After the marriage, Griffith and Johnson would go their separate ways and onto their own troubled lives. By this time, Griffith had slowly moved up the ladder to smaller parts in bigger films while Johnson caught pop culture lighting in a bottle when he did the wildly popular television series *Miami* Vice. Griffith slowly succumbed to the party lifestyle and the early stages of substance abuse while Johnson continued to carry on as the hot new king of celebrity Hollywood. And a bit of a Don Juan to boot.

Johnson would have a relationship with actress Patti D'Arbanville that would produce a child while carrying on a much publicized romance with mega star Barbara Streisand . Griffith would go the more traditional route, marrying actor Steven Bauer in 1982, a five-year marriage that would, likewise, produce a child.

Griffith and Johnson reconnected in 1989 during

a period when they had both done stints in rehab and were seemingly through with the Hollywood fast lane. Early in 1989, Griffith discovered she was pregnant with Johnson's child. Five months into the pregnancy, Griffith and Johnson married for the second time. This time the ceremony had a more serious tone. The consensus of those in attendance was that this time the vows would stick.

On the surface it seemed like the proverbial happy ending. Johnson and Griffith had seemingly gotten the partying and the substance abuse out of their systems and seemed determined to make a fresh start in their relationship and their lives. The fact that they were about to become parents was just the perfect beginning of their new life together. They both acknowledged their happiness in the days leading up to the marriage. To those who heard it, it did not seem like Hollywood smoke and mirrors. It all seemed very real.

So real in fact that, while Johnson and Griffith were occasionally spotted out and about during this period, the couple finally relocated to Austin, Texas in an attempt to avoid the crush of media interest and to wait out the final months.

Griffith would recall in an *US Magazine* interview that during her pregnancy she had withdrawn from work, preferring to spend her days with her husband on the set of *Miami Vice*, as she recalled, "being Don's woman." She was quite content. "It was great for that time but I would go crazy if that's all that I did," she told *US*.

On October 4, 1989, Dakota Johnson was born.

CHAPTER TWO
NAKED TO THE WORLD

If there was any hint of their former wild lives, the birth of Dakota quickly drove it out of them. As hard as it was for most Hollywood types to believe, the impact of their first child together was to put them in a state of domestic bliss. They were still Hollywood royalty but they were no taking giant strides toward being Middle America.

The newly married couple's first step after the birth of Dakota was to steer very clear from the glitz, glamour and, yes, temptations of Hollywood. They proved how serious they were in that regard by putting down $600,000 on a renovated three-story, 7500 square foot ranch style house in the suburb of Woody Creek, Colorado, just outside of Aspen.

Colorado at that time was considered a desirable oasis for those running from the spotlight and into some semblance of a normal life. People were seemingly smarter and more enlightened about things and the backdrop of mountain ranges, woods and grassy flatlands as well as the annual brush with snow and mother nature's elements, made for a place where prying eyes were rarely in evidence. It would not always be that way but, for now, it suited Don and Melanie to a T.

Johnson and Griffith's respective careers had plateaued at a comfortable level. Johnson had *Miami Vice* and the occasional movie to keep him busy while Griffith was, for the moment, a content stay-at-home mother. They were diligent in balancing work and family time. Melanie, with Dakota in tow, would occasionally travel to be with Don on the set of *Miami Vice*. But, for the most part, they became homebodies. It was a change in lifestyle that was abrupt but ultimately one that allowed them to settle into a family oriented, somewhat wilderness life.

And on the surface it all seemed to be working. Celebrity watchers had been certain that this change of life would not last long and that Johnson would be the first to crack. But the stories of the actor's wild partying life and numerous relationships had suddenly disappeared from the gossip landscape. What stories that did appear were usually warm and cozy puff pieces about Johnson and Griffith living the good life at Woody Creek. And in those stories there was much to talk about.

They rode horses around their sprawling 20 acre property and days were filled with family oriented activities. With Griffith getting primary custody of her son with Steven Bauer and Johnson's son with Patti D' Arbanville a regular visitor, their new life resounded with the sound of children's voices. It was light years removed from their former lives in Hollywood's fast lane but, in a very real sense, it was a non-stop party.

Griffith was very much the homebody during the first years of Dakota's life, working only when she felt the need and savoring the small moments such as when Johnson would return home after a hard day's work to be greeted at the door by Dakota rushing into his arms while Griffith would yell 'Daddy hug!' in the background.

Somewhat annoying to Griffith were her often vain attempts at keeping Dakota from crawling into their bed at night and curling up with Johnson. For his part, Johnson was an immediate pushover for his infant daughter, leading an amused Griffith to tell **US** "He's such a sucker for her. Anything she wants she will get for the rest of her life."

Needless to say, the Dakota as a toddler was the inevitable, precocious handful and, when added to the regular visits by their children from previous relationships, Griffith found herself very much in the mothering/nurturing state of mind. Prior to the birth of Dakota, Griffith had come to prominence on the strength of sexy portrayals in such movies as *The Drowning Pool, Something Wild* and *Body Double*. She would continue to get those kinds of offers and, while Johnson was fully supportive of her working whenever and in whatever she wanted, Griffith told *US* that she had, with the birth of Dakota, suddenly had a change of attitude.

"I would never do anything like *Body Double* now," she said. "It just wouldn't be right. In my heart and in my mind I've changed."

So much so that when she was offered a career making part in *The Grifters*, she politely refused. The part would ultimately go to Angelica Houston and would result in an Oscar nomination for the actress. Griffith admitted to *US* that she very much wanted to do that film.

"But that character was so evil and, without wanting to, you can bring a little bit of that character home with you. When I had Dakota, I just realized that wasn't the kind of person I wanted to be playing."

Occasionally the roles would be too good to resist and one in particular resulted in the young Dakota's first trip to Europe when Griffith accepted the role opposite Michael Douglas in the spy thriller *Shining Through*. It was a tough shoot...Late nights, cold temperatures and only seeing her husband a few days a month. But Griffith's spirits were constantly buoyed by the presence of her brood of children and, in particular Dakota, who indirectly, made her acting debut on that film when audio tracks of some very pivotal scenes had to be reshot when Dakota's frantic cries for 'Momma' turned up very clearly in the background.

Johnson and Griffith would set down deeper roots in the Aspen area when they enrolled their daughter in the private and very progressive Aspen Community School where Dakota made friends easily and, even in her first days in school, was as diligent as any pre-school student could be. But even at that very early age, those around her speculated that she would never quite get away from being the daughter of celebrity.

At a very young age, Dakota quite naturally gravitated toward the picturesque landscape, the snow-capped mountains and the sprawling countryside. The area was a haven for countless celebrities who had come to the Aspen area to escape the prying eyes of Hollywood. Consequently they tended to shy away from putting on airs and were down to earth in their dealings with each other. Even at an early age, Dakota become emotionally and spiritually tied to the area.

"It's home," Dakota fondly recalled to *Aspen Peak*. "It's a special thing to have had in my life."

From the outset, Dakota was a bright, inquisitive and spirited child. One moment she would be enthusiastically involved with her friends and the next quite content to be alone with her thoughts. In fact, her first memory of life in Aspen was very much in keeping with that youthful yin and yang as she explained to *Aspen Peak*.

"My first memory is of my fourth birthday," she said. "I was having a big birthday party and was taking a nap before it started. All these kids were jumping on a trampoline and I came downstairs in my pull-ups. I remember just standing there realizing my party had started without me. I loved growing up in Aspen. Especially in my early years."

It came as no surprise that Dakota was very much a child of fantasy and imagination. She would spend hours watching cartoons and fantasy/fairy tale style movies. She related to *The Hollywood Reporter* that she grew up on a daily diet of one particular Disney classic.

"I watched *Mary Poppins* every day," she reflected. "*The 'A Spoonful Of Sugar'* scene with all the drawers opening and the toys dancing around was the most amazing thing ever."

At a very early age, Dakota was also coming to grips with the fact that what her parents did for a living was something special. Many's the time that one or the other would be away from home on a film shoot or that famous names, which meant nothing to a four year-old, were brought up around the dinner table. Dakota would take it all in stride. And the reason being that celebrity life was not introduced with a lot of drama but rather in a low key, natural way.

"I'd watch my parents working on a film or television set but I wasn't sitting there, studying them," she told the *New York Times Syndicate*. "I was usually off playing with a production assistant. I led a pretty normal life. It was an average home aside from the fact that my parents were famous and we traveled a lot."

But it was to the credit of her parent's determination to keep their non-working lives normal that Dakota grew up feeling that there was nothing out of the ordinary in the family dynamic. Occasionally something would register, perhaps a newspaper photo or a conversation in which one of her parents had to go away to work but, even at that, it was always done matter of factly.

As she grew older, those talks would inevitably center on the occasional gossip or tabloid story. Johnson and Griffith would be quick to let Dakota know that sometimes stories about them were made up and that, if she wanted to know the truth, all she had to do was ask. It would be an enlightened form of parenting from two people whom you would never have thought would have that trait of parenting in them.

"For me, it was just my family," Dakota explained to *Interview*. "It's the way we grew up, just us kids and my mom and dad."

Dakota learned to be herself at the feet of her liberal post-hippie oriented parents. There was never any pressure to be an actress or anything else beyond a normal child. And when she quite naturally developed a childlike interest in dance, which often saw her practicing spins and twirls around the family home, it was enthusiastically encouraged. She would acknowledge years later in a conversation with UK Journalist Matt Mueller that she often felt "like a dreamy kid" during her childhood years.

"I started dancing when I was very young and would keep dancing for 12 years," she told *Aspen Peak*. "When I was young that was really my thing."

As was Dakota's early introduction to the concept of not wearing clothes.

"Growing up, it was such a task to put clothes on, and when I did, I'd look like such a crazy person," Dakota told *Details*. "My parents would be like, 'Dakota you don't have to wear tights and jeans and a skirt.' Being naked was just more comfortable and my mother was like 'Alright. Do what you gotta do'."

Dakota would defend her parent's seemingly overly permissive attitude as just their reaction to the way she quite naturally was in a conversation with the *New York Times Syndicate*. "According to my mother, I was a complete wild child. I was a little bit recalcitrant growing up."

Dakota's 'wild child' appearance extended to her rather unruly, yet striking, mop of white-blonde hair. "I didn't brush my hair," she told journalist Matt Mueller. "I had this tangled white-blonde hair and it was like, 'Nope, I'm not gonna do it.' I've had a weird life, a very different upbringing."

The early years in and around Woody Creek and Aspen were a quiet, idyllic and nurturing time for the young Dakota. Her parental ties to Johnson and Griffith were traditional and strong, but often challenging as Johnson would explain in an interview with television talk show host Tom Snyder.

"My sons were a lot easier to get through to than my daughter. She seemed to have my number. She could just run through those numbers."

In years to come, Dakota would always marvel at the level of interest people had in her growing up the daughter of two famous people. "It was weird that people were so interested in what it was like growing up," she explained to the *New York Times Syndicate*. "They would get mad at me, disappointed in me and happy with me. They'd cheer me on and ground me just like normal parents do."

But for Dakota and the rest of the family, the good times would be relatively short-lived. Barely three years into their marriage, Johnson and Griffith were having problems, specifically Johnson. The temptations of the Hollywood high life proved too much for Johnson who returned to his drinking and partying ways. At one point in his downward spiral it was even rumored that he had fathered a child with another woman while on a Toronto film shoot. He eventually realized that he once again had a problem and went to rehab in an attempt to once again clean up his life.

At age three, it was most likely easier to tell Dakota that her father was off working and she was more inclined to believe it. However Dakota was a bright child and so it was a safe bet that she was sensing some discomfort in the family dynamic.

Johnson would emerge from rehab full of promises to stay straight and to turn his life around. Griffith was torn in the face of her husbands' statements and seeming sincerity. It was the classic tale. She wanted to believe Johnson in the worst way. But in her heart she secretly knew better.

Griffith lamented the gradual disintegration of their marriage and foreshadowed its eventual demise in an interview with *Vanity Fair*. "Don is no angel," she said. "He's not easy. It's hard for me to imagine life without him."

Griffith put up a continued, supportive front as her husband battled his demons. She wanted a life with him, for herself and for Dakota and the other children that had become a part of their world.

But for Griffith it had finally become too much to bear and, in 1994, the couple divorced for the second and final time. Although only four years-old at the time, Dakota was well aware of the tensions in the household and, although she had no idea about what divorce was all about, she was stoic in looking back on those tough days with *Access Hollywood*.

"I got to experience a lot of things that a lot of people don't get to experience," she said. "There were times that were really difficult. But I think those times just made me a better person."

By 1995, the fantasy dream house in Woody Creek Colorado sat empty. The next phase of Dakota Johnson's life was about to begin.

CHAPTER THREE
IN TRANSITION

Griffith did the best she could to ease the pain of her children in the wake of her divorce. They remained in a much down-sized residence in the Aspen area for a time and, in an amicable gesture, allowed liberal visitation for Johnson with the children.

Consequently Dakota, while occasionally sad that she would not be seeing her father on a daily basis, seemed reconciled to the divorce and, according to observers, was fairly well-adjusted throughout the early days of her parent's split. Griffith, on the other hand, was devastated and, in a classic divorce scenario, blamed herself for much of the divorce. She would say to whoever talked to her in those dark days that she vowed to not get into another relationship until she was happy with herself.

That decision would last less than a year.

In the meantime, Dakota continued to grow emotionally. The seeds of 'whatever,' perhaps the result of the divorce, were fully formed in the young girl. There never seemed to be extreme highs or lows in Dakota's world. That she would go through those post-divorce days as if nothing had happened was cause for some concern that she was holding her feelings in. People were quick to judge Dakota's attitude as something of a self- defense mechanism induced by scars from the divorce. But, at her young age, her attitude certainly did not run that deep. She simply felt safe and secure in her world and was mentally and emotionally playing it day by day.

Griffith continued to work and found what she perceived as the perfect cure for the blues, a light-hearted romantic comedy called *Two Much*, starring opposite Latin heartthrob Antonio Banderas and Darryl Hannah in a tale of a musician involved in a love triangle with two sisters. *Two Much* was essentially predictable fluff. There would be no acting plaudits but it was a paycheck and something to keep her occupied. What she had not expected to find in the Latin star was that the romantic sparks in the script would translate into lust and love in their real lives.

Two Much was not the first time Banderas had laid eyes on Griffith. Six years previously, as the actor recalled in a *Hello Magazine* chat, both had been in attendance at Oscar ceremonies in which Griffith was nominated for the film *Working Girl*. "I saw her at the Oscars. I didn't know who she was but as soon as I got out of the car, I saw her. She was gorgeous. I'll remember that day my entire life."

For Griffith, who at the time was going through a rough patch in her divorce with Johnson, it was quite literally love at first sight as she gushed to *Hello Magazine*. "The first thing he said to me was he wanted to know how old I was."

Banderas, who was also in the midst of a messy divorce, was likewise smitten. He was instinctively drawn to her shy seductive nature and quiet assertiveness.

Not long after they began their affair, Griffith discovered that she was pregnant. It was then that she discovered that her lover was truly a man of principle and character. The couple were married in May 1996 and Stella Banderas came into the world in September of the same year. In a matter of months Dakota now had a stepfather and a half-sister in her family circle.

Rebound relationships, in and out of Hollywood, had a spotty track record. Throw in a half sibling and it would seem that Dakota most certainly would rebel against the emotional turmoil and a new parental figure in the house.

Fortunately Banderas would turn out to by the ideal person to take on a family of children of many past relationships as well as their own child. He was aware and patient, a gentle guide rather than trying too hard to be their friend. This was particularly true when it came to the daughter of Melanie's relationship with Johnson and Johnson's love child with Patti who had become a *defacto* member of the family and who visited regularly.

"They've suffered," he told *Hello* in reference to their dealing with their parent's divorce and splitting their time between them. But he acknowledged in the most loving way that all the children in this current relationship were his children. "When I talk about them, I say my children, not my stepchildren," he told *Hello*.

The next few years were a kind of feeling out process as Dakota got to know her new stepfather and her sibling . At this young age, Dakota was very flexible to the changes in her life and adapted fairly easily to the mixed nature of the new family.

Dakota would attend Aspen Community School up until the fourth grade, continuing to be alternatively a gregarious and solitary child. And while she had never been overtly guided in the direction of an acting career, her continued interest in dance resulted in appearances in several school plays including *The Nutcracker* and to her way of thinking, even at the ripe old age of eight, her imagination and an interest in ways of expressing it were growing by leaps and bounds.

"As a child I was into all sorts of activities and I thought about being lots of different things," she offered in an *American Profile* item. "But the one thing that stuck with me and that made sense to me was telling stories."

Dakota would get her first chance to be an actress at age nine in what would turn out to be a family affair in the movie *Crazy In Alabama*. This tale of an abused wife who runs off to Hollywood to become a star while her nephew deals with a racially motivated murder by a corrupt small town sheriff had all the makings of a dark and surreal comedy drama. It was one of those neither fish nor fowl stories that is death in the highly commercial movie industry prone to taking very few chances. But it struck a nerve in Griffith's creative soul. *Crazy In Alabama* was something she just had to do.

After securing the film rights, Griffith ran up against the reality of securing funding for a film that, at best, might break even. She also saw it as an opportunity to bring her family closer together.

Griffith turned to Banderas to direct her. It was a risk, personally and professionally, for Banderas who would make his directorial debut in directing his wife. As an extra added attraction, the couple decided that their daughters, Dakota and Stella, would play small parts as the daughters of Griffith's character.

Blurring the lines between reality and fiction was something that Dakota, despite her young age, instantly latched onto in the role of Sondra and, in her scenes with her real life mother, Dakota would showcase a quite natural affinity for the camera, projecting some enjoyable and, yes, believable moments as the perky and precocious daughter. *Crazy In Alabama* would go on to only do marginal business upon its release in 1999 but it cemented young Dakota's childish but earnest aspirations to make a life for herself in a fantasy world.

"It just made sense to me that I would be acting and being in this business," she told *American Profile*.

But rather than rush headlong into the acting life Dakota, either because of her age, by design or her parent's dedication to letting their children have a normal life, did nothing else remotely entertainment-related for the next couple of years. Because of her parents' respective careers, Dakota and her siblings became nomads of a kind, shuttling back and forth between Aspen and Los Angeles and accompanying her parents on far flung filming locations and soaking up the day to day vibe of being in the company of filmmakers. Although still a pre-teen, Dakota was instinctively aware of the desire to, somehow, be a part of this world.

Especially since to her way of thinking she was

not good at much of anything else as she explained to UK journalist Matt Muller. "I was never good at anything. I was never great in sports. I was never good in school."

Nor did the young child feel, even at that young age, that she had much of a sense of humor. "I never thought I was funny," she confessed to *Vanity Fair*. "I never thought I would do anything that had to do with comedy."

And it went without saying that Dakota's liberal/borderline permissive upbringing had much to do with her growing sense of independence. Because of the family's globetrotting ways and various children from various relationships, it was not uncommon for Dakota, even at a fairly young age, to be separated from her family.

A case in point being when Dakota turned eleven. Griffith and Banderas were off on one of their regular trips to Spain about the time Dakota was scheduled for two weeks of summer camp in Carmel Ca. Mother and daughter went their separate ways without a second thought. After Dakota was finished with her summer camp, she was met by her nanny, put on a plane and sent off to join her parents on the other side of the world. Griffith did not for a moment fear for her daughter's safety during their separation, telling the *Los Angeles Times* "She must be having fun because I haven't heard a word from her for two weeks."

At age 12, she tentatively put her toes back in the entertainment water when she agreed to do a photo shoot of 'Celebrity Kids' for a spread in *Teen Vogue Magazine*. For Dakota it was harmless fun and an opportunity to hang out with other children of celebrities. And she was the first to admit that attending the glitzy *Teen Vogue* party at the high-class Chateau Marmount was an amazing experience.

And it was an indication of just what kind of life Dakota was leading. By the time she had reached the fifth grade, formal education was largely a figment of the past. Seemingly always on location or travelling with her father, mother and stepfather, Dakota had fallen into a pattern of tutors and homeschooling that would prove nothing more than a stopgap bandage to her waning interest in education. When her father landed yet another long running TV series *Nash Bridges*, which filmed in San Francisco, Dakota's time with her dad was enhanced by her daily trips to the set to watch her dad work and the opportunity to explore the city.

Eventually Johnson and Griffith came to the conclusion that their daughter was at an age where she might need a little stability in her life and so Dakota was enrolled in a high-end Catholic boarding school for high school age girls. Rather than balk at the idea, Dakota seemed to think being in an all-girls school would do her a lot of good. But, as she recalled in an *Elle* magazine interview, that feeling did not last too long.

"I was just miserable there," she said. "The girls in that concentration were just too horrific."

Dakota wanted out. So she called her dad. Johnson came to the school and whisked her away. Another example of the power Dakota had over her father. She would often smile at the mention of just how easy it was to get her father over a barrel. And simply point to her face.

Dakota's mother and stepfather would settle more permanently in Los Angeles by 2003 and she would settle into a more formal and agreeable educational life in the New Roads School. The private institution was known for its more creative curriculum and Dakota enthusiastically embraced this free spirited environment, enrolling in drama and dance classes and honing her budding acting skills in many productions. It was most likely this immersion that contributed to her now well-formed desire to be an actress.

Dakota adjusted to her life at New Roads with relative ease. She would make informal friends as most teens do, easily and naturally. She was popular among her classmates not so much because of her celebrity parents as her innate ability to be laidback and positive.

"She was just a beautiful person," described Sarah Mintz longtime a friend and filmmaker in an interview with *Cosmopolitan*. "We met through friends and then through high school for a couple of years. We were close but never what you would call tight knit friends."

Sadly the specter of having celebrity parents also followed Dakota to New Roads and would often see the young teen bullied by fellow students. Dakota would painfully recall in an *Elle* interview some years later that classmates would often greet her by waving newspaper gossip clippings of her parents in her face. "I think people, especially the press, like to pick on the children of famous people," she said. "I think that's fucking awful. Things get made up and there's nothing you can do as a 16 year-old. You're like 'What the fuck did I do?'"

Dakota would acknowledge during a press junket interview for her television series *Ben and Kate* some years later that there had been other potential outlets for her creativity while at New Roads. "I took visual arts and figure drawing in high school and, for a while, I thought those were the areas in which I would make a living. I probably would have done that if I didn't already have the drive to be an actress."

Despite speaking to his daughter often, Johnson would recall in an interview on *The Jay Leno Show* that he had no idea that his daughter had designs on going into the family business. "I didn't know any of that," he said. "I wasn't aware of her taking acting classes in school or any of that. Eventually she called me and asked my advice on what she should do in certain situations and that's how I found out."

Dakota went through a normal adolescence. She had her crushes on celebrities and, more realistically, on boys her own age. The conversations with her mother on such matters were, like everything else in their relationship, straightforward and honest. It's a safe bet that conversations between mother and daughter were less about the birds and bees as they were about the facts of life.

Dakota's first real relationship was with budding musician and classmate Noah Gersh which began when Dakota was 16. While on the surface it seemed like the typical high school romance, the couple seemed the ideal match emotionally. As befitting a musician, Gersh was focused and serious about his goals.

Although already leaning in a creative direction, Dakota remained emotionally all over the place. Gersh would be Dakota's anchor for her remaining years in school and for some years after. Dakota would state on several occasions in the years ahead that Gersh was a stabilizing and calming influence on her and had a major impact on her beginning to focus more on what was important to her and less on what people around her expected.

In a quote that appeared in her *IMDB* page as well as several other sites, Dakota recalled that her teen years were definitely a time when she turned to the arts. "I felt so much when I was fifteen, sixteen, seventeen," she said. "I felt everything. I didn't understand (myself). I was so happy and yet so angry and sad. That was the point when I realized that I needed to tell stories and make characters come alive. I needed to make people cry and make people think and make people angry and happy and make people laugh."

For his part, Banderas was intuitive when it came to what was going on with his step daughter in a conversation with *Hello Magazine*. "She's got her mind set on so many things at once. Everything is moving at breakneck speed for her."

Ultimately Dakota's parents would be comfortable with her hopes for an acting career. After all, they reasoned, being the parents of celebrities and seeing firsthand what went into their acting careers had been the best kind of education. Melanie, in particular, reasoned in a *Los Angeles Times* interview that her children "had seen so much that nobody was going to fool them or trick them."

Johnson saw his daughter's most certain odyssey into the 'family business' on a more philosophical level borne out of a long standing attitude that his children were imbued with by Griffith and himself as they grew older.

"We always had this saying in the family," Johnson said in an interview with television talk show host Graham Norton. "You're on the payroll as long as you go to college or something like that. If not, it's over, you're on your own, get a job."

Consequently Dakota went into 2006 with eyes wide open, when she was approached by The Golden Globes to be that year's Golden Globes' Girl. The Golden Globes, made up of foreign press, had over the years become the more fun counter to the often stodgy and serious Oscars. And part of the blatant courting of celebrity favor had always been to have the children of notable actors and actresses on stage during the ceremonies, handing the prized awards to the presenters and acting as eye candy as they ushered presenters and award winners off stage in a timely manner.

And there was more than a little history involved in selecting Dakota. Melanie Griffith, on the strength of her association with her mother, Tippi Hedren, had been a Golden Globes' Girl in 1975 and had assured her daughter that it would be all glitz and glamour and that she would have a lot of fun being in the spotlight for the very first time. Dakota readily agreed to do it.

But in looking back on that night, she discovered that being a Golden Globes' Girl was anything but fun. "It was terrifying," she explained to *Starpulse*. "You bring the Golden Globes out and you give them to these very talented people. I was 16 and I was terrified. I was wearing these gloves and I kept thinking that they (the awards) were going to slip out of my hands. I was going to be the girl who dropped a Golden Globe on the stage and ruin everything. I don't even remember the night because I was so terrified.

Dakota also recalled that her job that night was to make sure that the presenters were camera friendly. "You have to move everyone and you have to make the presenters move back to a certain line so their nose isn't in the camera during their speech.

"It was such a job."

The Golden Globes would officially usher Dakota into the Hollywood fast lane. She was suddenly being invited to places she had never been and to parties that would last until all hours. She was 17, the daughter of celebrities and was now, in the eyes of many, a budding celebrity in her own right. It was her ticket to ride.

And over the next year she would ride the train hard.

CHAPTER FOUR
THE HIGH LIFE

But it would all go pretty much unnoticed.

Dakota was the soul of discretion when it came to her social life. Who she hung out with and who she partied with was a secret that few, given her stature in Hollywood, were interested in investigating. Depending on who one talked to in the tabloid press at that time, she was either Dakota who or Dakota who cares.

With her parents regularly out of state for a film and the lions' share of the supervision in the hands of nannies, it was a safe bet that Dakota could easily slip into her home at any hour of the day or night, in just about any degree of intoxication, and into her room. After the fact there was also the speculation that her parents' liberal attitudes, especially Griffith's, would have made any public confrontation of her partying a minor blemish easily dismissed or talked out.

Once the press got beyond the fact that she was the daughter of Don Johnson and Melanie Griffith, she was still largely an unknown. To the point that even the most knowledgeable paparazzi would often take her picture on the street and then remark 'who is that?'

It was the same with the party life. Those in her tight circle knew that Dakota was slowly but surely evolving into a 'party girl' and that excessive drinking and drug use were now a part of her lifestyle. But if one were to scan the press clippings of the day between the years 2006 and 2007, there was nothing to indicate that Dakota had a problem.

Until Dakota turned 18 in October 2007.

Johnson and Griffith's relationship had remained amicable post-divorce and so it was not surprising that both were in attendance at their daughter's birthday festivities. Their casual conversation at the party reportedly turned to their daughter and the fact that Dakota had been partying non-stop for the better part of a year.

They sensed what was going on. After all, both of them had a history of overdoing it and so they could easily see the signs. Shortly after their conversation, they sat down with Dakota and laid their concerns on the table. Dakota agreed that she had been overdoing it and that, yes, she had been drinking and doing drugs. Typical of the family's upfront interactions, there was reportedly no heated arguments or denials. Dakota and her parents calmly agreed that she should enter rehab.

And so, literally in a stealth maneuver that caught the Hollywood media completely off guard, Dakota entered the Visions Teen Treatment Facility in Malibu Ca. for a 30-day stay and would follow that up with a period of outpatient treatment in a facility in Brentwood, Ca. In a story by *The National Enquirer* that laid the whole situation out to the public, it was also reported that Dakota was also attending Alcoholics Anonymous meetings.

In later years, Dakota would vehemently deny *The National Enquirer* report. Yes, she had been in rehab but it had been for therapy to deal with some issues she was having with her parents. Although she would never be specific as to the issues, she would often acknowledge in later years that being around her parents had, in a sense, forced her to deal with adult, real world issues before she was ready.

Not that she had been totally blindsided by the idea of being the offspring of celebrity parents who, to varying degrees, were notorious. But she had become annoyed and defensive as she had gotten older at the constant prying into what it was like growing up the child of Don and Melanie. But, as she explained in a quote that appeared in her *IMDB* web page, she was, to a degree, willing to go along with it.

"It's not necessarily annoying," she explained. "I've come to understand the allure of that to other people and how it seems so interesting and different. It doesn't really bother me because I get it. But sometimes it is kind of a drag to talk about."

According to the follow up reports, Dakota, despite continuing to deny the reason behind her rehab stint, quit her alcohol and drug consumption quite easily and was once again on the straight and narrow path as she contemplated her final year at New Roads School.

But fate, and perhaps a bit of help from her parents, became a belated birthday gift when Dakota came to the attention of high octane modeling agency, IMG. Reportedly the agency had put her on their radar following her Golden Globes appearance but had waited, in that time honored modeling way, to step in and proclaim her their 'next big thing.'

Speculation immediately appeared indicating that IMG was throwing Dakota a bone based on who her parents were. Dakota could not have avoided hearing those comments but by now she was well versed by her parents on how even the hint of celebrity can bring out the naysayers and the best way to deal with media stories was to ignore them. In that sense, Dakota had learned her lesson well. But at the end of the day, while legally an adult, emotionally she was still very much a typical teenager who was plagued by insecurities and doubt. For Dakota, entering the adult world and a celebrity driven one as well, was shaping up as a true challenge.

As it turned out IMG was not in the habit of doing anybody favors.

The agency had been instantly drawn to her youthful yet classic features and those provocative pouty lips. She was fetching in a muted 90's techno brat sort of way and it went without saying that Dakota did photograph very high class. The consensus of those who saw her early portfolio of images was that one could put Dakota in just about anything and she would look hot.

It went without saying that Dakota was naturally photogenic. There was nothing forced or put on to her look. It was all a natural by-product of the free and open way she went about her life.

IMG would sign Dakota shortly after she completed her stint in rehab and the 18 year-old would enter the first true phase of her professional career. She was captivated by the glitz and glamour of the big time modeling and fashion world. But what was immediately telling was the fact that she also paid attention to the mechanics of it all, the lighting, camera angles, the details of a photo session. Dakota, to her own way of thinking, was not the typical model. And in self-assessment, she would maintain that she was sticking to creative integrity through it all when she talked to *Aspen Peak*.

"I'm excited about modeling," she said. "But modeling for me is not all about the fame and the clothes. For me, it's about expressing oneself."

Dakota's first assignment as a model was truly a heady one, a big splash in the pages of *Vogue Magazine,* supervised by no less a light than famed fashion icon Andre Leon Talley. Dakota would often recall the shoot as an exciting and surreal experience in which she soaked up all the nuances, professionalism and, of course, the glamorous clothes that were part and parcel of her maiden voyage into the modeling world.

"It was all so surreal," she recalled to *People*. "The fact that I was doing *Vogue*. It didn't really sink in until afterward."

However even in those intoxicating moments, Dakota would concede to *The Daily* that it was only a momentary oasis in her world.

"I'm very excited about all this," she offered. "But I still have to go back to California and finish my final year of high school."

Dakota would continue to work sporadically as a model throughout her senior year. And it was not always glamorous, working long hours under hot lights at the whim of often demanding photographers on such lesser known jobs as modeling for top designer Thankoon Panichgul's more commercially-oriented ready to wear line. But she maintained a professional yet realistic attitude, considering it a glamorous job but, in her eyes, just a job.

"The modeling was fun but it was never what I loved," she told *Interview*. "It was simply about having fun and paying the bills."

And paying her own way was her reality. Her parents had stuck to the edict that once she went her own way in the world, no help from them would be forthcoming. Rather than complain that the security blanket was being pulled out from under her, Dakota was quite happy to be truly on her own and justifying her creative endeavors with a paycheck.

While she would continue to plug away at her senior year at New Roads School, her first modeling assignments and the endless creative possibilities that lay ahead were a constant distraction. She had come to the conclusion that any further education would be arts-oriented.

After a diligent search of schools that would satisfy her creative urge, Dakota settled on the famed Juilliard School, which was known for a performing arts curriculum designed to turn out polished performers. In short order Dakota applied to Juilliard and received an invitation to come and audition for admission. On the day in question, Dakota showed up for her audition and, as she explained to UK journalist Matt Mueller, immediately realized she had made a huge mistake.

"I was waiting to do my audition and I was talking to one of the students who went there and he was like 'It's great! We're here every day from 9:00 in the morning until 11:00 at night, and then on the weekends we have groups and we work on our scenes.' I was just like 'Fuck that! When do you get to be a human?' "

Dakota's rejection of Juilliard was also pretty much a blanket indictment of what she considered her formal education. For Melanie, this pronouncement had not come as a surprise. "She hated school," she explained to *Extra*. "By the time she had reached the 11th grade, she was telling me, 'I'm going to be an actress.'"

But it was more than just being an actress. Melanie acknowledged in *Extra* that by the time she was finishing high school, her goals as an actress were, for Melanie, seemingly getting personal and perhaps a little closer to the emotional bone. "She said 'I'm going to be really big. I'm going to be bigger than you.'"

CHAPTER FIVE
COMING OF AGE

Dakota immediately put Juilliard out of her mind and returned to New Roads for the final months of her senior year. At this point, she was secure in the knowledge that saying thanks but no thanks to Juilliard was the right career move. The Juilliard experience also blunted her desire for further formal education. Dakota would go on to finish her final months at New Roads and that would be it.

But Dakota was nothing if not a realist. She was more focused than ever on making it as an actress and felt that some additional training outside of the formal education she had received would help her round the learning curve.

Enter Tom Todoroff.

Todoroff was a free thinking actor/writer who had made his name in the industry with a naturalistic teaching style that allowed his pupils to organically discover their true talents and cultivate them. He had also become the go-to guy when reigning superstars wanted to guide their children into the family business. Over the years Todoroff had taught the daughters of Robert Wagner and William Shatner and, he recalled in a 2013 interview with the author, "I taught Angelina Jolie before she became Angelina Jolie." He seemed the ideal choice for Dakota.

Dakota came to Todoroff's attention in 2007. In a similar fashion, it was at the behest of a family member, in this case, Dakota's half-brother Jesse, also an actor. Todoroff, who had worked, coincidentally, as a producer on the movie *Tin Cup*, which starred Dakota's father Don Johnson, recalled that Dakota entered his world far from the cliché celebrity sibling that was notorious in Hollywood and who Todoroff had encountered often over the years.

"Dakota felt like she needed acting lessons," he recalled. "Coming from a family that's in show business with Don and Melanie, it would have been very easy for her to think 'Okay I'm in California, take a few lessons and get on a sitcom or something.' From the beginning, what I loved about Dakota's attitude is that she was willing to put in the work as if she didn't have any celebrity ties. She needed to immerse herself into this. It couldn't be superficial."

Dakota would attend Todoroff's class for a period of one year through 2008 in Santa Monica, Ca. It was a class made up primarily of what Todoroff described as "a lot of people who were young, really wanted to work and tended to want to be real actors." And he would find out during a preliminary meeting with the budding actress that she was all business.

"Dakota immediately got that there was work to be done," the instructor recalled. "She was young but she was ready to work really hard. Quite simply, she wanted to learn. Dakota would not have any problems learning the way I teach. She had a real sense of what she was getting into and that was good enough for me."

Todoroff came away from that preliminary interview with Dakota pleasantly surprised. "I could see that, at a very young age, she had a lot of confidence. She came into my class with a level of confidence that somebody in their teens doesn't normally have. Dakota had a real point of view from the moment I met her. She was like, 'This is who I am' and she just put it out there."

Once it became known that Dakota had signed on with Todoroff, there was the inevitable speculation that it was only a matter of time before the diva in Dakota, as well as a sense of entitlement brought on by her celebrity parents, would begin to show itself. However Todoroff said that during the year Dakota was a pupil, nothing could be further from the truth.

"She grew up around it [celebrity] and, by virtue of her wanting to come and train, that told me that she was not a diva. Her attitude seemed to be that people were going to look at her with a lot more scrutiny because of who her parents were and so she had better be serious about this. She came in with the attitude that she could not ride on her parent's coattails."

During her year with Todoroff, Dakota mixed well with her classmates who, according to her teacher "Everybody found her immediately adorable and very funny."

That she fit in did not tempt Dakota to cut corners in her education. If anything, the ease in which she assimilated into the social fabric of fellow actors only made her more serious about learning the nuts and bolts of her trade.

"She was very beautiful to behold but she worked

in my class as though she did not have an overt consciousness of that," said Todoroff. "I've found that beautiful people like Dakota tend to work as though they're 400 pounds and have one eye in the middle of their forehead."

During her year in the class, Dakota was diligent in her studies. Whereas some would occasionally balk at Todoroff's reading list as part of the curriculum, the young actress would spend her time away from class immersed in the theory of her chosen craft.

"She was really open to the way I taught," reflected Todoroff. "Dakota was very disciplined and open to everything she was getting from myself and the other actors. That's the way she came in the door. There was a real spontaneity with Dakota to go with whatever was happening. I know she has said that she never had a comedic sense and for me that was just part of the charm. She did not realize that she had that in her and I saw it all the time."

Dakota's year with Todoroff concluded midway through 2008. Quite naturally Todoroff saw the year as the first step in what he predicted would be a very long career. "There was never a moment where I thought she had arrived and that it was time to go. That's what I liked about her. When I would see her work in later years, what I saw did not surprise me. It was like 'yeah, that's Dakota.' "

Dakota would, likewise, look back on her studies with fond memories of her coming out in her first steps in the direction of being a well- rounded actress.

"Tom Todoroff's class is amazing," she reflected of the experience to *Aspen Peak*. "Expressing yourself through acting is incredibly satisfying."

By the time she had matriculated through Todoroff's approach to acting, she had gathered a level of skills that, no doubt aided and abetted by her parentage and modeling experience, made her desirable to the established Hollywood acting community. During her modeling days, there had been a sniff of interest in Dakota as an actress but she had declined on the grounds that she was not ready. Shortly after graduation from New Roads School and the conclusion of formal acting classes with Todoroff, the prestigious William Morris Agency signed Dakota up as a client.

Not surprisingly, Dakota took the signing to William Morris with equal parts excitement and realistic expectations. She was excited at the possibilities but also quite uncertain of her talents and the ability to function as a professional actress.

Conversations with her parents, as well as her stepfather, were encouraging. They explained to Dakota how important William Morris was in the entertainment industry and how a literal Who's Who of legendary actors had been the agencies' clients. Those conversations also instilled in her the fact that she should not expect too much too soon.

In the world of William Morris, newcomers were usually brought along slowly with small parts in medium to big budget films and, a bit further down the line, bigger roles in smaller, independent films. For her part, Dakota was not in any big hurry. She was young, attractive and totally receptive to the idea of being patient in a whole new world that was opening up to her.

Besides going into 2009, she already had a lot on her plate to keep her busy.

The Mango Jeans line had long been a plumb assignment on the international fashion scene. To be considered the face of Mango was, in most quarters, an indication that a model had truly arrived on the scene and was worthy of celebrity consideration. Shortly into the New Year, it was announced that Dakota had been selected to be the 'Face' of the latest Mango collection. Dakota had already had some experience working with the fashion industry on an international level and, in particular, was looking forward to working with famed Spanish photographer Txema Yeste.

One of the perks of modeling on an international level was the opportunity to see the world. Dakota's experience in Spain would be no exception. Having travelled there on several occasions with her mother and stepfather, Dakota knew a lot of the places to go. But it was her spirit of adventure that served her well during this latest tour, exploring non-touristy streets and shops and finding a real sense of herself as a true free spirit.

Through the famed photographer's lens and guiding eye, Dakota in tight jeans was a joy to behold. For the shoot, she would advance the notion of model as defiant rock chick, striking provocative and alluring poses, showing just the right amount of skin and presenting a classy, yet tattered and raw showcase for the Mango line. Dakota saw the Mango photos as a step forward for her career and said as much when she told *Fashion United,* "It's been an honor to work with Mango. I think their collection is great. It's very chic and elegant while, at the same time, cool and casual."

On the personal front, her relationship with Noah

had survived their graduation from New Roads. With their respective careers beginning to flourish, the couple moved easily through the days, comforting and encouraging each other, enjoying nights out and just as joyful peaceful evenings at home. To that point they were the prototypical love match.

In Dakota's world the future looked bright.

CHAPTER SIX
MOMMY'S ALRIGHT

Dakota knew the score.

She had grown up with parents who had been very open about their addictions and stints in rehab. It was that straightforward approach, two years earlier, that had helped her deal with her own demons. So even as her modeling career began to take off and she was moving on in her own life, she was well aware of what was going on at home.

And that her mother was having problems.

Griffith, who has had a history of alcohol and drug problems going back as far as 1998, was on a skiing trip in 2009 when she injured her knee. Doctors prescribed painkillers as part of her treatment and it was not long before Griffith relapsed once again into addiction. Banderas was soon aware of his wife's renewed addiction issues and, as he explained in *AARP The Magazine*, it went without saying that the children would know as well.

"The pretending is the worst because the kids are so smart," he said. "They can see through all of those things and, if you don't talk about the problems, it creates a very dark place."

With that attitude, it was not long before both Dakota and younger sister Stella were aware of what was going on with their mother. And one day they sat her down and forced her to face the facts.

"It wasn't an intervention, well sort of in a way," Griffith told *The Los Angeles Times* of that day. "My daughters really sat me down and said, 'Look Mom, this is what it is.' They were the ones who said you really need to get help. And I heard them and knew exactly what they meant."

Shortly after this conversation, Griffith checked herself into a rehab clinic in Utah. It was a difficult process, made all the easier by the fact that Dakota, Stella and Banderas were at her side several times a week with words of love and encouragement.

Griffith would emerge from rehab, clean and, to date, has not relapsed into addiction again. She gave all the credit for her recovery to her daughters. "I couldn't have done it without them," she told *The Los Angeles Times*.

CHAPTER SEVEN
SEX ANYONE?

Shortly after completing the Mango job, William Morris landed Dakota her first acting role since her childhood part in *Crazy In Alabama*. It was time for Dakota to sleep her way into the public consciousness.

By the time Dakota heard that she was being sent out on an audition for *The Social Network*, the movie was already shaping up as a sure fire bet come Oscar time. The story, the founding of Facebook and the personal and professional fallout that resulted in a flurry of lawsuits, was first rate, up-to-the-minute and hit the teen-young adult demographic right between the eyes.

The pedigree of the project was palpable. It was studded with names from top to bottom. Director David Fincher. Screenplay by Aaron Sorkin. The cast was frontloaded with young Hollywood types that included Jesse Eisenberg, Andrew Garfield and Justin Timberlake. In was the kind of film, according to the buzz, that could easily make even the most miniscule role, a career changer.

Which was exactly where Dakota fit in. The character she was going up for, a quirky 'of the times' coed named Amelia Ritter, seemed on the surface to be yet another female cipher, the loose girl who sleeps around and does not have a cogent thought in her head. But Dakota, ever on the lookout for nuance and depth in everything she did, saw the role differently.

"I play a Stanford coed named Amelia Ritter," she explained to journalist Mark Mueller. "She's highly intelligent and kind of quirky. She's amused by the whole concept of going to a party, bringing a guy home, waking up the next morning and going, 'So who the fuck are you?' "

She was also quite intrigued at the prospect of working with such an A-list cast and director right out of the box, even if her role was basically a glorified cameo.

But rather than the obligatory bedroom romp, Fincher, equally adept at matching his actors with challenging moments, had something more in mind for the admittedly small scene. Dakota's entry in *The Social Network* begins the morning after as she confronts the sleeping Sean Parker (Justin Timberlake) and in a pithy back and forth, the film establishes Parker as the founder of Napster, a pivotal turn in the storyline.

And it was a scene that was ultimately played largely for laughs as Dakota recalled. "We skipped the sex scene part," she told Mark Mueller, "and started with the whole morning after. It introduced Sean Parker in a totally goofy sort of way. Working with Justin Timberlake was just so funny to me. But he was so sweet and professional."

In a scene that lasted slightly under two minutes, Dakota, dressed in red underwear and a long shirt, was immediately impressive. Her modeling background served her in grand fashion with subtle turns and head movements. Her timing and exchanges with Timberlake came across quite naturally. And it went without saying that Dakota was sly and sexy to the camera eye.

This was Dakota's first brush with big studio filmmaking and she would find that, even in her very small moment, everybody was extremely professional. Fincher was alternately straight to the point and a slight bit humorous as he guided his two actors. Timberlake, who after making a name in the world of music was now attempting the same in film, talked easily with Dakota between takes but was, likewise, intent on the scene at hand.

Director David Fincher had nothing but praise for the actress and her *The Social Network* role during a promotional trailer for the film that aired on YouTube and elsewhere. "It was a pretty thankless role. But we needed somebody who would be pretty unforgettable in the scene that introduced Sean Parker. In a weird way she tells us more about Sean Parker than a lot of people in the movie do. She wanted him and she seduced him without knowing who he is. I felt the scene with Dakota was such a wonderful way of showing how charming Sean can be. It's not his fame that gets this particular girl. It's only in hindsight that she says, 'So that's who you are.' She's just wonderful here."

Tom Todoroff recalled in a 2013 interview that he had the occasion to see *The Social Network* not long after its release. He had no idea that Dakota was in the movie. "But then all of a sudden it was like, 'that's Dakota!' She was right there. A lot of times an actor will go into a scene opposite a big star and it's like, 'Oh it's Justin Timberlake' and the other person just hands the scene over to the star. Dakota didn't do that. She didn't look up or down. She met him eye to eye. I was so happy for her. She did a solid job and she held her own. As a teacher, I live for moments like that."

Word of mouth quickly spread along the critical grapevine that Dakota had not only stolen the scene from Timberlake but, in her limited capacity, had turned in one of the most impressive, nuanced acting turns in the film. Director Fincher would ultimately pay her the highest compliment when, as remembered by Dakota in an *Interview Magazine* interview, "When I did *The Social Network* he told me that I managed to make a thankless role pretty awesome."

Flush with good notices for her work in *The Social Network*, Dakota was immediately caught in the fantasy that she was a real actress and that a lot of people would see her. Not surprisingly, reality soon set in and the initial rush of a job well done was replaced by the expected down time. Dakota was anxious to spread her wings, creatively, and that did not necessarily mean in a commercial arena. Through her group of friends and those she had come to know in the industry, Dakota made it clear that she was up for any work that would challenge her.

That's when old friend Tyler Shields entered the picture. Shields, a former professional skater turned avant-garde photographer, had been part of Dakota's growing circle of creative people since 2007. He recalled in an interview with the author in 2013 that Dakota, in a creative sense, seemed to him somebody that was always ready for a new challenge.

"We were always talking about movies and the idea of working together on something," he recalled. "She loved the idea of doing something truly epic."

Shields, who has become known and notorious, for depicting blood and violence in his work, prided himself on being an immediate judge of character. He sensed that Dakota was smart and that her long-standing relationship with Noah pointed toward stability, another plus in Shield's ledger.

"You can tell when you meet someone, who has it and who doesn't," he said, "and Dakota definitely had it. She didn't have a drug problem, she came from a good family and she liked to work hard. In that sense, Dakota was a no-brainer."

Shields had been around the young Hollywood crowd long enough to have encountered the children of celebrities before and so barely blinked an eye when he had discovered who Dakota's parents were. "I never really thought about that when it came to Dakota. I don't really care who someone's mom and dad are. Who Dakota's parents were had nothing to do with who Dakota was."

And who Dakota was, according to Shields, somebody who was not willing to play it safe in the wake of making a big splash in the blatantly commercial *The Social Network*. "The way I approached things did not put her off. She was totally into it. She wanted to push the boundaries."

And so, post *The Social Network*, Dakota and Shields sat down to talk about doing something that the photographer hoped would be an offbeat post card in what he perceived as a fast rising career. "I wanted to make something huge so that when she became huge, people would want to look back on this video before she blew up."

A literal home video, clocking in at a minute, five seconds, was conceived and executed over a period of one hour at Shield's home. In keeping with the photographer's modus operandi, grim and gruesome and often very violent, Dakota, dressed in a bathing suit and looking dazed, confused, psychotic and truly creepy, does a truly upsetting pantomime in which she moves slowly while bringing hands caked in blood to her face and slowly smearing it on her face as her face does a silent, painful turn. Adding to the horrific imagery was a close up of Dakota in anguish, her teeth chattering in a near sardonic smile.

"It was already pretty cold when we shot it," recalled Shields, "and just when we began shooting I covered her bathing suit in ice to add to the effect. Dakota was truly freezing. Her reaction was so intense. She was so good. She was really pushing herself. Those are the people who really do their best. You can't be scared in this business or you are just boring. On that day, Dakota just had it. Whatever that 'it' is, Dakota just had it."

Dakota's collaboration with Shields would become an immediate hit on the underground Internet circuit. It is a small project that rarely gets mentioned in stories or her biography and there were certainly those who warned that the Shields video might come back to haunt her at some point. But Dakota was not concerned. The 1:05 second video was a true expression of her artistic and individual stance in the world. And she was proud of it.

Dakota had been immediately taken with the

filmmaking process and the fact that her mere two minutes on screen in *The Social Network* had resulted in such a positive response. She immediately made it clear to her agents that she was up for more and was soon in another audition room reading for a much more substantial part in the romantic teen fantasy *Beastly*.

In this modern take on the classic tale of Beauty And The Beast, an arrogant, spoiled high school rich kid embarrasses a girl with a supernatural trick up her sleeve. She turns him into an ugly, scarred creature and admonishes him to find love within a period of time or he will remain ugly forever. *Beastly* was targeted directly at the teen/young adult market and as such was cast very young with a list of hot and handsome teens that included Alex Pettyfer, Vanessa Hudgens, Mary Kate Olson and such TV-friendly actors as Lisa Gay Hamilton, Neil Patrick Harris and Peter Krause. On paper, *Beastly* was the ideal template for the PG-13 market, made quickly on a reasonable budget and destined to make the majority of its money in the first ten days of release in mega-plexes all over the country. But for Dakota, there would be a diamond in the rough.

Dakota would take on the character of Sloan Hagen, the girlfriend of the pre-transformed Beast. Again on the surface, another seemingly cliché role. Spoiled, entitled and rich. Dakota felt she was more than capable of connecting the dots. But as she would discover, there was more to Sloan than just another long suffering girlfriend with little or no character. And with her intuitive nature as her guide, Dakota immediately saw 'room to move' within the seemingly stock nature of her Beastly role.

"Sloan is with Kyle [the male lead] at the beginning of the movie and, in a sense, she's very much the female version of Kyle," she offered in the film's production notes. "She doesn't seem to care what is said about her because, in her world, everything that she is, does and says is cool. It's only after Kyle disappears from her world that Sloan comes to realize the negative effect he had on her."

Armed with the character's psychological depth and how what she perceived as a nuanced performance would add depth, Dakota was confident the day she would go into the audition room to meet with director Daniel Barnz. And, as he explained in the film's production notes, he was duly impressed.

"Dakota came into the audition and she immediately grabbed us. She read the lines and I immediately said, 'We've found our Sloan.' "

And what Dakota found as filming on *Beastly* commenced was that the potential for her character at the script stage arrived as a full-bodied anti- hero of the first order. In the final stages of development, Sloan had evolved into a full blown, self-centered head case who lived in a world where to cheat and to be cheated on was all merely part of the pampered and spoiled job description.

"I'm pretty much an al -around asshole in *Beastly*," she told Matt Mueller. "It was fun to be the mean person. It's so opposite from who I am. It was mini-skirts and matching outfits and makeup. I looked like such a prissy bitch."

However looking the part was only the tip of the iceberg for Dakota in the film. The director and fellow cast members would constantly marvel during her three weeks on the set at how she could instantly morph from the Dakota that everybody liked a lot into somebody who they could instantly loath. It was not too far a stretch for those who saw *Beastly* to give Dakota major acting points for turning Sloan into somebody they could easily dislike.

To this point, Dakota had been getting her feet wet in small, fairly stock roles in conventional, commercial mainstream films. But the artist in her was chaffing at the prospect of exercising some internal demons in something a bit deeper and off beat. She would find that in an offer to play one of the leads in *Savage Innocent*, the latest project by controversial filmmaker Larry Clark who had made his bones on such dark and psychologically ambiguous films as *Kids* which inevitably took the teen rite of passage to a very dark place. And Dakota was instantly attracted to the storyline.

Savage Innocent tells the story of a mysterious Latin boy who appears, one day, naked on the streets of Brentwood, Ca. The boy is befriended and taken in by a rich family. The plot deepens as the boy falls in with an underground fight club where he becomes a world beater through a strange style of fighting that incorporates fighting moves and bites that are very dog like in nature. Through it all, the mystery of just who the boy is and where he came from remains uppermost.

Not surprisingly, *Savage Innocent* would have a checkered history. Reported start dates were all over the place. At one point the film, then titled *El Santo*, was set to film in Mexico. By the time Dakota, as well as actors Ray Liotta and Rory Culkin, were on board,

Savage Innocent, reportedly with a budget of $3.5 million, was given a start date in Los Angeles.

All of a sudden, the film literally disappeared off the radar. It is doubtful that *Savage Innocent* was ever made and none of the actors list the film on their respective filmographies. It was an anecdote that would rarely turn up in Dakota's bio and then it would only be little more than a title. And so while enticing, Dakota had learned a reality of the movie business...

And that was not every film that gets green-lighted gets made.

CHAPTER EIGHT
BELOW THE RADAR

Dakota was working fairly regularly into 2011 and there was already a hint of a buzz around town. But, for the most part, the young actress continued to move largely out of the public eye.

Her by now live-in boyfriend Noah and she would occasionally be spotted on the street by paparazzi as they walked down the street, into a restaurant or the occasional movie. But the few token camera clicks by the shutterbugs were non-intrusive. To their way of thinking, Dakota was not yet marketable enough on the world pop culture stage to warrant much more than a few shutter clicks. The paparazzi were after the usual tabloid darlings and bigger game and Dakota did not qualify as either. Consequently even the slight interest was rare as the couple were basically homebodies who spent much of their together time ordering in take out, watching a movie or just plain talking.

At a time when most of young Hollywood was just now entering the Hollywood fast lane, Dakota had seemingly already outgrown the Hollywood lifestyle and had thrown all her energy into her work and finding work. She would often acknowledge in interviews that she was essentially lazy and that, when not working, was more inclined to sleep.

Dakota's dalliance with the press was also running contrary to many of her peers. The tabloids would occasionally run a picture but there was never anything really meaty to write about. On her worst day, Dakota could not compete with Lindsay Lohan for the media's attention. The actress was doing more interviews and, in that realm, had morphed into a cordial and concise starlet, still projecting an image of a real life girl who was making her way in Hollywood without causing any screaming headlines.

With such a miniscule resume to this point, Dakota's encounters with the press would inevitably revolve largely around her celebrity parents and what it was like to grow up with superstar parents. For the most part, Dakota would be patient with those questions, acknowledging that once you got past her limited acting and modeling experience, there was not a whole lot to talk about. Occasionally she would good naturedly bristle at talking at length about her family, such as the time she quipped to *California Lifestyle Magazine,* "I didn't choose my parents."

Being the spawn of celebrity was having its own challenges when it came to the day to day hustle in highly competitive Hollywood as she explained to *Variety.* "When I was first starting out, people, especially industry people, would have the attitude of, 'Do you think you can really do this?' But it's gotten a lot better. People have started to understand that I'm from a creative family and that this is the kind of work that works for us."

While weighing an increasing number of film offers, Dakota continued as a much in demand model. Her often provocative look found a home in 2010 when Australian clothing designers WISH brought Dakota down under for a shoot to highlight their new 'Rising Star Campaign.' As the photos indicated, Dakota had quickly become the consummate professional. She struck the ideal poses, was on time and never displayed even a hint of ego. But even as the praise for her modeling acumen poured in, inwardly Dakota was chaffing at the idea that, at that point, she was considered a model/actress. A big part of her wanted the model part to go away.

Her next step in the direction of Hollywood came with the offer of a small support role in an art house driven character film entitled *For Ellen*. The film, directed by independent favorite Soo Young Kim and starring Paul Dano, focused on a struggling musician, his impending divorce and a sudden urge to reconnect with the daughter he really never knew. *For Ellen* was, from its inception, a small film and, by association, her character, Cindy Taylor, was primarily on the edge of the main story, appearing in a dream-like flashback of the male lead's high school days and first love. Her moments on the screen were soft, sentimental and poignant and showed, if nothing else, that Dakota was capable of subtlety.

Admittedly, Dakota did not have a lot to do. But the mere fact of being on location and watching as the cast and crew pulled this labor of love together for very little money was an education in the reality of the business that she soaked up. Following on the heels of big budget studio films *The Social Network* and

Beastly, the bare bones and very naturalistic nature of *For Ellen*, was a definite and productive change of pace.

The *For Ellen* experience whet her appetite for more work that was independent minded. Dakota made it clear that she would favor a substantial role in a small film, at this point, then window dressing in a big studio film. But she also made it clear that whatever offer was presented to her, she would be up to the task, showcasing the long held Hollywood acumen of saying yes to everything.

But within the context of Hollywood, she remained particular at what she said yes to. She had a good relationship with the William Morris Agency and had made it plain what she would and would not do. First and foremost the film and her character would have to offer acting challenges and not just clichés. And Dakota knew the difference because she would read every script that was offered her from cover to cover.

As it would turn out, the next offering, *Chloe and Theo*, would be another small film with a substantial acting upside. *Chloe and Theo*, a spirited and slightly offbeat look at hopes and dreams, was shaping up as one of those feel good movies of years gone by. An elderly Eskimo makes his way to the big, bad, cynical city and, through adventures and misadventures, brings joy and hope to a group that were emotionally and otherwise burned out on life. The fact that it was just as much a comedy as it was poignant drama was right up Dakota's alley.

The young actress played the character of Chloe, a spirited homeless girl who comes under the mysterious Eskimo's spell and ultimately is an important element in his turning around the other denizens of the city. Dakota related to *The Last Magazine* that her impression of *Chloe and Theo* was that the movie "Was about relationships and how people are treated."

"I researched the homeless in preparation for the role," she continued. "Previously the homeless had been invisible to me. But this project has made me much more conscious of everyone."

A big part of Chloe's character was the fact that she was obsessed with the late martial arts star Bruce Lee. She recalled in *Interview* the intense research she put in to believably portray that one character trait.

"I learned everything, read everything and watched all his movies," she laughed. "I tried to get some friends to watch the films with me but nobody was interested. So I ended up watching all his films alone. Doing it that way kind of added to the obsessive nature of Chloe."

The hard work would pay off in Dakota's most impressive and sustained performance to date. As one of the pivotal leads, she was on screen for much of the movie. And rather than just playing the limited and very brief role of a cipher, Chloe allowed her many acting turns, from bright and spirited to hopeful to determined. Although the movie is just now making its way to the mass audience, it was something that Dakota could look back on as an understated but breakthrough moment in proving to the doubters that, yes, she could indeed act.

CHAPTER NINE
NEXT STEP

Perception is everything in Hollywood. And in many quarters, Dakota, following the critical response to *For Ellen*, was now considered part of a never-ending group of young, attractive Hollywood starlets making the endless rounds of auditions and figuratively scratching and clawing for every part. Being part of the crowd was a crown that Dakota did not easily wear. Anybody who even hinted at the 'struggling actor' tag was in for a rebuff, albeit a mild one.

Dakota was insistent in a 2012 interview at The Sundance Film Festival that she was not a part of a group of always desperate and hungry actors. "For me it's all about the art and the process. I don't feel like I'm in competition for every part. Right now I'm just moving from film to film, looking for the best parts for me. I would like to do a TV series at some point but right now I'm just concentrating on films."

That Dakota would even hint at the idea of suddenly dropping the role of legitimate film actress in favor of the grind that was a weekly television series caught many media observers by surprise. Despite a lot of quality television being created of late, television was still considered, in many quarters, to be the place actors went when their film career was in decline. In the case of Dakota, they failed to take into account that the actress was simply casting a wide net for the best possible work, period. Dakota was simply playing by her own rules.

But early on, more than one filmmaker looked beyond her perceived talent to potential stunt casting. One of the more serious attempts was director Sean Baker who, at the time, was casting around for a small generational comedy called *Starlet* in which a young girl and a much older woman make each other's acquaintance after which laughs, hijinks and heart emerge. Baker had the bright idea to cast Dakota and her grandmother Tippi Hedren in the lead roles. It all seemed a natural right up to the point where Baker had a change of mind and looked elsewhere.

Dakota found the ideal next project for her creative leanings in the slightly out of kilter coming of age film *Goats*. *Goats* follows the life of a 15 year-old boy who, after living with a new age divorced mother and a wise sage called Goat Man, is ready to leave this unorthodox nest and make his way as a student at a prestigious prep school. What he discovers is the reality that he is not emotionally equipped to deal with this new world. *Goats*, directed by Christopher Neil and starring Graham Phillips, David Duchovny, Vera Farmiga, Ty Burrell and Keri Russell, featured Dakota as the young boy's first flirtation, a yoga obsessed, spirited wild child named Minnie.

On the surface, Minnie appeared a variation on the character Dakota played in the film *For Ellen*. But as she explained in a conversation with *In The Maxx*, the setup of the film and her character made the role ideal for her creative approach to her acting career.

"There's a lot of components to this film," she said. "It's about all these characters finding out what's important to them in their lives. Yes this is a coming of age film but it's different in that it focuses on what goes on in between their lives. Minnie is sort of a controversial character, somebody people would have normally immediately made their minds up about. I wanted to give the character sweetness and make her loveable."

Minnie in Dakota's hands were just that. The tentative courtship between her and the boy were played out in soft gazing moments and enticing interplay in which both characters approach just how far they can take things and what lines should and should not be crossed. Their subtle dance would prove to be one of the more endearing elements of the film.

Goats, much like her everything she had done since *The Social Network*, would fall prey to typical independent film realities, low level distribution deals that, if lucky, would get the film into a handful of theaters and garner enough favorable press to jumpstart a DVD release some months down the road. Ultimately Dakota was getting good notices in movies that only a figurative handful of people were actually seeing. On a certain level it was frustrating to the actress. But it was not the kind of frustration that was keeping her up nights. Ever the positive soul, Dakota saw only possibilities and potential in even the smallest victories and stood ready for whatever came next.

It would be inevitable that with her growing prowess as an actress capable of different turns and shades of emotion that studio projects would come calling. Such was the case when Dakota was offered the part of an undercover cop named Fugazi in yet another movie reboot of a vintage television series, in this case a comedic updating of that 80's chestnut, *21 Jump Street*.

Dakota took the job with a grain of salt. She knew this major studio release would reach a wide audience. She also knew it would be very commercial and nowhere near serious art. But at that moment, she was looking for something light and easy. "This movie is bringing back funny and goofy," she said in a You Tube video. "It's giving me the opportunity to do something ridiculous."

The role would offer little in the way of real acting challenges as Dakota was required to do little more than to play the foil of the film's two main lead actors Jonah Hill and Channing Tatum. But it did allow the actress to showcase her budding comedic skills.

"My character is an undercover cop who is highly competitive," she said of Fugazi in a *Celebs.com* interview. "She's a bad ass. She thinks the two undercover cops she's working with are lame and she gives them a bunch of crap and makes fun of them."

Despite being less than enthusiastic about her modeling career, which was slowly taking a backseat to her film work, Dakota realized that, on a certain level, she had emerged as a much sought after type, sultry and provocative in a slightly retro way. It also did not hurt that, at her level in the fashion industry, the money was quite good. Her popularity in that arena was apparent shortly after her turn in *21 Jump Street* when, in the space of a month she landed the coveted assignment as the face of Uniqlo, a Japanese clothing line and headed up the ad campaign for Oliver Peoples, a California based eyewear company.

However Dakota remained ever on the alert for acting projects that would challenge her. She came about just such a project in a horrifically bent and hilarious comedy send up entitled *All That Glitters*, directed by the always controversial literary and film maven Bret Easton Ellis of *American Psycho* fame.

Reportedly conceived as a short film but ultimately an homage to a short lived cult TV series of the same name, *All That Glitters* is an equal opportunity joke, a spoof of rich teenagers with no morals and the seeming never ending parade of television shows portraying teens and young adults, *All That Glitters* was a no holds barred laugher that gave Dakota a bigger than life, caricature to play.

"I played Danica French," she explained in the releasing company, *Funny or Die's* promotion video. "I'm the villain and I'm very rich and spoiled. My character is an aspiring fashion designer who spends most of her time having sex and taking club drugs."

All That Glitters was a fun filler that had achieved some level of a cult following on the *Funny or Die* website. And for those who had seen it, the spoof showcased Dakota as a deft hand with broad/ham fisted comedy.

Dakota was seemingly at a crossroads following her latest modeling duties and the filming of All That Glitters. She was increasingly in demand on both fronts. To make the next big step, she would most likely have to ditch one and go full steam into the other. Although there would still be the high profile modeling assignments, Dakota did not waver in her drive to be an actress.

Now it was only a matter of what came next.

CHAPTER TEN
GOOD FOR A LAUGH

Dakota would be the first to tell you that when it came to comedy, she was a zero.

"I never actually thought that I was funny," she confessed to *Vanity Fair*. "I never had comedy training or improvisational training of any kind."

Which is why she was constantly amused at the number of auditions she was sent on that revolved around getting laughs. Dakota was often amazed that she would actually land the part. One part she did not get was in late 2011 when she was sent in to audition for a recurring role in the cable comedy series *Girls*.

Girls had class written all over it. The premise of young girls wandering through their lives in the big city had immediate pedigree. It was the creation of the new 'all world' talents of Lena Dunham and was being ramrodded by the comic genius of Jud Apatow. Dakota knew the producer by reputation and was shaking in her boots when she went to audition.

"I was terrified," she confessed to *Vanity Fair*. "I was reading for his associates and he [Apatow] was sitting quietly in a corner. At one point he said 'go' which was his way of saying to play with it and to improvise the material. I had not done any improvisation before so I just started saying a lot of stuff off the top of my head. I don't remember what I said but I remember I had a pretty active imagination at that time. Unfortunately I did not get the part."

But it would not be the last time she would have contact with him. Not long after the Girls' audition, Dakota was sent up to another Apatow project, *The Five Year Engagement*. The film, which top-lined Jason Segel and Emily Blunt, chronicled the comic trials and tribulations of a couple who are madly in love and plan to be married but only after a lengthy five year engagement that will allow them to get their professional lives in order. Needless to say laughs and chaos ensue. Much of which centers on Dakota's character, Audrey, a trifecta of weird, annoying and sex-obsessed who becomes the Segel character's girlfriend during a downturn in the titular couple's relationship

Dakota recalled in an *Interview Magazine* conversation that the audition for the Judd Apatow co-production was a lot less stressful than her *Girls* experience. "The casting director called me in to read with Jason [Segel] and then a week later I got the part."

A part that at first glance appeared daunting to the comedy shy Dakota. The script, co- written by Segel and the film's director Nicholas Stoller, was improvisational heavy, the type of story that would cause actors to think at lightning speed in developing believable character arcs. Dakota's concerns were quickly alleviated during her first meeting with Segel and Stoller.

"I've never had training in improvisation," she told *Details*, "and the script was basically all improv. It was like 'Okay you guys are the best and I've never done that'."

But the filmmakers were insistent that Dakota was the right person for the job.

"They told me what they wanted the base of the character to be," she related to *Interview*, "and then they gave me a lot of free range to do what I wanted. Obviously they use improv a lot so I was pretty much able to create this character on my own."

And in Dakota's hands, Audrey emerged as, possibly, her most fully realized creation to date. The restaurant hostess, in the actress' mind, emerged as an engaging mixture of flamboyant and sympathetic. A literal force of nature that pursued Segel's character sexually and, in her own weird, lighthearted and demanding way, made her a controlling presence. Audrey ultimately emerged as an important adjunct to the main storyline.

And it was Dakota's willingness to let it all hang out, emotionally and creatively, that gave free reign to a character that could have been mere cipher in less capable hands. Even the sex scenes with Segel, which emerged as hilarious as well as telling insights into character, were something that played to Dakota's strong acting instincts.

"Those things [the sex scenes] are always a little uncomfortable at first," she told *Interview*. "But the whole point of the scenes is just to show how ridiculous this girl is. So I made a complete fool of myself. It's a lot more fun to do things like that when you don't care what you look like."

Dakota would finally acknowledge in a *Woman's Wear Daily* story that her character in the film was, in a sense, a driving force by virtue of her unpredictability. "The character I play is really weird and really comfortable," she said. "My character was supposed to be really too young for him and so he was really uncomfortable all the time."

Following on the heels of *The Five Year Engagement* and *21 Jump Street*, Dakota was suddenly being perceived as a classic comic foil. But rather than as a cliché sidekick for mindless teen exploitation pictures, filmmakers were getting Dakota. Yes she could do comedy. As long as it contained some kind of edge.

And when the script for *Gay Dude* (aka *Date & Switch*) came her way, Dakota liked the film's intent and spirit. Two guys about to turn 18 vow to lose their virginity at all costs seemed like a very pat and, perhaps an exploitive, idea in the time-honored tradition of such romps as *Porkys*. But there was an enticing twist to this film directed by Chris Nelson, written by rising star Alan Yang and starring Nicholas Braun, Hunter Cope and Dreama Walker.

One of the two friends suddenly decides to come out of the closet and let the world know that he is gay. For Dakota's part the character of Em, the intended girl one of the boys hopes to lose his virginity to, circles the pair's sexual conundrum, providing the expected sass, spirit and tease, admittedly more of a cliché role than anything else given the film's broad, comedic nature, yet continuing to play to Dakota's strengths as a performer who could make the most obvious characters enticing and watchable.

In the wake of *Gay Dude*, Dakota had slowly but surely emerged in Hollywood circles as an actress who could add substance, believability and versatility to just about any role. *The Social Network* and *21 Jump Street* had given her the most exposure and had been obviously commercial successes. But to many she remained a slight blip on the Hollywood horizon. Her strongest exposure had come in films like *The Five Year Engagement* and *Chloe and Theo*, the former on release would do moderate business while *Chloe and Theo*, to many her most well rounded performance to date, barely registered in the movie going audience's consciousness. Once you got outside the very tight knit Hollywood film community, Dakota was still considered a B-level actress at best.

Consequently while many held out belief that she could truly carry a big studio film on her own, the nuts and bolts, bottom line attitude of the industry still registered a big question mark on Dakota's ultimate bankability and her ability to open a film.

To her credit, Dakota was either oblivious or uncaring about the dollars and cents of Hollywood. She was content with being a true artist and was in no hurry to see her name up in lights. Despite the corner many observers felt she was being painted into, Dakota remained confident that her time would come.

As these things often happen in first relationships, Dakota and Noah slowly but surely began to drift apart. No reason was ever given for the end of their relationship but the obvious culprit, to those who made a living speculating on such matters, was the fact that while Noah was beginning to gain some small level of recognition as a musician in progressive/independent circles, Dakota's much more rapid career arc had quickly eclipsed his. And as often happens, the couple were spending more and more time apart. There were no screaming tabloids and breathless gossip accusations to document the breakup. Like every other element in Dakota's life, the relationship had quite naturally run its course. Dakota felt the expected sadness in the wake of the breakup but she had her work to distract her. She was not in any hurry to fall in love again.

Dakota had essentially been naïve when it came to love and romance. She had stated over the years that she preferred long-term relationships. And while she did not rush into another relationship, being suddenly single and out in the Hollywood night life suddenly made her the target of gossip and innuendo. One of the more amusing tabloid reports, not long after her breakup with Noah, had the young actress reportedly romantically involved with *Brokeback Mountain* star Jake Gylenhall. It was a report that everybody in Dakota's circle had a good laugh at and her publicist readily denied.

The reality was that she had met him at a party and talked with him briefly. And in Hollywood that's all it took to conjure up the image of Dakota rushing into a rebound relationship.

In the face of often absurd headlines, the reality was that Dakota had cultivated a rather low key lifestyle when not working that seemingly precluded even a tabloid hint of romance. In a *USA Today* interview, Dakota was self -effacing as she described what she did for fun.

"I sleep a lot," she laughed. "I'm tired all the

time. I love eating. And I love shotguns. I don't shoot at actual animals, just clay pigeons on sporting days. For some reason, I started doing it recently and I was pretty good at it so I just kept going."

But Dakota would remain nothing if not consistent in her drive and ambition. This first slate of films had moved her slowly but surely into working actress mode and there were many who were predicting stardom in her future. However Dakota was more than willing to bide her time and wait for the next opportunity.

2011 moved inexorably into 2012. For Dakota it would be business as usual.

CHAPTER ELEVEN
HIT THE SIT COM

By the time Dakota signed on the bottom line to play the title character of Kate in the Fox television situation comedy *Ben and Kate*, the show, in typical Hollywood fashion, had been through a number of changes over the course of its six-month odyssey.

Since October 2011 when Fox first indicated an interest in a pilot for the series, the show had gone through three name changes, the hiring and firing of two show runners over creative differences and the casting and, in one pivotal case, the recasting of a character. Originally *Saturday Night Live* alum Abbey Elliott had been picked to play Kate. But, after what it referred to in the Hollywood process as a pre pilot "table reading," it was suddenly decided that Elliott, 24, was too young to play the role. Three days after it was announced that Elliott had been dismissed, on March 23, 2012, Dakota was announced as the new Kate.

Doing a weekly television series, and particularly one that would test her comedic chops, had been on Dakota's wish list from the beginning. Most actors would look at the opportunity as a steady and possibly long running gig, with good money and residuals for eternity. Typical of Dakota, all she could think about was the chance to test her skills and to do some good work.

Dakota recalled in a *Zap2It* conversation that landing the role of Kate was a whirlwind affair. "I read the script one night and was won over by the crazy nature of the script. I went in the next day and read for them [the producers] and was offered the part by evening. It's really bizarre because you hear these stories all the time but they never happen to you. And this all happened in less than 24 hours."

Once she got over the initial excitement of landing her first prime time television show, reality set in for Dakota as she realized that a lot was riding on her being very good. "I was selected only a few days before the pilot was shot and I knew a lot of people were putting a lot of blind trust in me," she told the *New York Times Syndicate*. "Kate and I were completely different. I'm not even close to being a mother."

Ben and Kate, reportedly based on the true life adventures of producer Dana Fox and her brother Ben, told the story of a very serious single working mother, Kate, who unexpectedly has her lighthearted but ultimately underachieving brother, Ben, move in with her and her daughter. As planned, comedic chaos ensues as the mismatched brother and sister learn to live together and hopefully learn from each other. Admittedly the concept, while cute, was not blazingly original and would ultimately live or die by the stories and the actor's ability to bring something fresh to the table.

For Dakota, *Ben and Kate* was a big step on several levels. It was her first television series and her first as the lead. To this point in her career, her film roles and modeling assignments had been loosely scheduled and had allowed for requisite downtime for Dakota to catch her breath. By contrast, weekly television was a notorious grind in which rigid schedules and long hours were the order of the day. A point that would be driven home to Dakota almost from the start.

"The hours are insane," she reflected to the *New York Times Syndicate* during a momentary break in filming the show. "It's physically taxing. I'm on my feet 14-16 hours a day. I have to remember that I have a life and a family and that I have to call my mom back."

And as she explained on the *Elliot in The Morning* radio show, these were all big concerns. "I'd never done television before and it was all very intimidating and intense at first. All I knew for certain is that I wanted to do the best work that I possibly could."

There was also the fact of adjusting to the idea that *Ben and Kate* would not merely be an appearance and then done. If, as everybody hoped, *Ben and Kate* turned out to be a ratings success, Dakota could be working with her cast and crewmates for a number of years. Dakota was pragmatic in discussing that issue with *Hit Fix*. "I think that when you know that you might be around these people for a while, you tend to find things to like about the people you're working with. And with this cast, that's been easy."

The *Ben and Kate* pilot was picked up by Fox and

production on the series began on May 9, 2012. Many were surprised that, at a time when the mortality rate for new series was high and few made it through a full season, Fox made a fairly unheard of announcement that they were committing to 19 episodes. All of which put even more pressure on Dakota who admitted to *Hit Fix* that her character was in a state of transition in her own mind.

"Kate's a fun mom but she's serious," she offered. "She's a single working mom who spends all her time and energy raising her daughter. At first, she's not really good at having fun. But the character is evolving and so I'm starting to get more comfortable with her."

She likened her character to the classic Lucille Ball in *I Love Lucy* as a template for her character in *Ben and Kate* in an interview with *Zap2It*. "We wanted to make it clear that Kate is smart and is a good mom. But she's also not afraid to look stupid or be goofy, funny or klutzy. I want women to feel that they know someone like Kate."

With *21 Jump Street* and *The Five Year Engagement* behind her, Dakota offered that a daily shooting routine that gave the actors room to creatively move, was easy to transition into as she explained to *Elliot in the Morning*. "For me, it's comfortable improvising on the show," she said. "We've created a routine on the show. First we shoot a scene as it was originally scripted, then we go back and shoot it again, sometimes adding new jokes and, sometimes, the actors just play around with the scene and see what they can do."

Ben and Kate moved like clockwork through

summer and fall of 2012. Dakota had adjusted to the beat of television production and, when not on the set, was usually found in and around Hollywood, shopping, in restaurants, hanging out with friends, or, as she was fond of saying, just sleeping.

The one thing that had suddenly changed was, as a star on a network television series, she was now very much in the public eye. Her comings and goings, no matter how mundane, began to make headlines in the tabloid and gossip press. And with that higher profile came the paparazzi. Dakota and the aggressive breed of celebrity photographers were not totally alien to each other. But the reality was that up until *Ben and Kate,* she had been more or less an afterthought. Now she was faced with meeting the often renegade and aggressive photographers on a near daily basis.

"Except for the paparazzi, people don't really recognize me," she disclosed in a *Toledo Blade* article. "Even if they do, hopefully people will just treat me as a normal person."

Dakota seemed comfortable and accommodating to the advances of the celebrity photographers, always seeming to have a bright, yet shy smile for the camera as she walked by. And by being accommodating and non- argumentative, she had gained a modicum of respect from a hard bitten group that regularly courted the abuse that was heaped upon them. Being in the public eye for much of her life was most certainly paying dividends.

It was during the run of *Ben and Kate* that Dakota and old school chum Sarah Mintz reconnected. This time in a professional way. Mintz, who was making her own way as a filmmaker while attending Tish

University, was in the pre-production stage on a short film called *Transit*. The film was a coming of age drama about a young girl who, after being abandoned by her father, ends up at a youth hostel where she subsequently faces her demons and learns about herself through interaction with the people she meets.

Mintz recalled in a *Cosmopolitan* interview that she had been monitoring her old friend's career from afar. "I knew she had done some things but had not really broken out yet. But I was pretty sure something big was going to happen for her and so this was my time for me to work with her,"

Dakota was in New York at the time and, although still in the midst of a grueling schedule with *Ben and Kat*e, for Mintz it seemed the perfect time to approach her old friend. She thought long and hard about how to approach her before ultimately deciding that the straightforward approach was best.

"I felt I had to impress her," Mintz related in *Cosmopolitan*. "We met and I sat there and explained why I thought it was an important movie to make, why I wanted her for the part and how I knew she would be the character I wanted. She said yes on the spot."

Transit was shot at a renovated motel in Malibu Ca. on a miserly seven-day shoot, a shoot that would coincide with her duties on *Ben and Kate*. Dakota knew that helping out Mintz would make for some very long days jumping back and forth between the two projects but felt strongly enough about *Transit*'s story and character to willingly take on the extra burden. Mintz recalled that the working dynamic between the two women was free and easy with the pair spending a lot of time just talking about life and how her feelings would strengthen the *Transit* story and character.

"She was funny and very self-deprecating, "Mintz told *Cosmopolitan*. "There was no pretention about her. I felt that she was all there and definitely listening."

And, as it turned out, Dakota was very much her own woman when it came to the particulars of a nude shower sequence and love scenes. "Dakota insisted on a closed set when we shot those scenes and had approval of anyone who would be on the set," Mintz related to *Cosmopolitan*. "There was definitely nudity that we could have gone further with and Dakota was fine with that as long as it was tasteful."

By the time *Ben and Kate* went on hiatus in December, the show was on the proverbial bubble. Critically the show was faring quite well. Ratings wise? Well that was a whole different story. People were tuning in but not at the numbers that the network was hoping for. The rumors began circulating that Ben and Kate was hanging on by its fingertips and that cancelation was imminent. But Fox insisted in public statements that they were quite happy with the show and that there were no plans to cancel the show.

Dakota made the most of her month long hiatus, vacationing in New York and in Aspen. Dakota at leisure was a completely different person, always at ease and always with a smile on her face. In the classic sense, when Dakota was not working, she was psychologically at ease in her world. If the media was aroused at the prospect of *Ben and Kate* being canceled at any moment, her immediate employment future was definitely not keeping her up nights.

If she was concerned about the fate of Ben and Kate, she was not showing it. "I don't really know when security happens," she told *Elliot in the Morning*. "I'm really happy doing this show. But if it gets canceled, I'll simply move onto the next thing."

Ben and Kate was officially canceled on January 25, 2013. True to her word, Dakota was almost immediately on to bigger and better things. Professionally...

...And personally.

"I'm not sure where I'm going to be tomorrow," she summed up her philosophy in a conversation with *People*, "or even in a week."

CHAPTER TWELVE
NEW KID IN TOWN

Dakota was never one to flit aimlessly from one guy to another. After her break-up with Noah, she had been in no hurry to start a new relationship. But that did not mean that she was not open to occasional flings and, in one case, a dalliance of the celebrity kind.

Sometime in 2011, Dakota was introduced by a mutual friend to the much older actor Stephen Dorff and, as detailed in a story by *Showbiz Spy*, the couple carried on a short and guarded affair before breaking it off. The relationship with Dorff was, in fact, so clandestine that it would be 2014 before even the slightest scraps of information emerged.

But midway through 2012, tabloid reports began to emerge that indicated that the young actress was once again seriously involved.

Dakota remained coy in the face of the growing gossip speculation. She indicated in a *Mail Online* story that "I do have a boyfriend that I have been with for a while." But she inadvertently fueled the fire when she refused to name him. But well into 2013, pictures posted on the internet, showing Dakota and her new guy together at parties and openings, just hanging out and, in one instance, intent on doing a crossword puzzle, made the rounds and the cat was out of the bag. Dakota did in fact have a new beau.

His name was Jordan Masterson.

Masterson, the son of an Australian rugby player and part of an acting family that includes brothers Danny (*That 70's Show*) and Christopher, is, like Dakota, an actor on the rise, having appeared as a regular in the television series *Geeks* and in the film *The 40 Year Old Virgin* among other television or movie credits. On the surface, Dakota being with a new guy did not seem so unusual. Actors and actresses, in an often cloistered Hollywood environment, rarely dated outside their circle. But there was one element in Masterson's background that immediately caused eyebrows to arch.

That old devil Scientology.

Masterson was a Scientologist. His parents were both Scientologists as were his siblings. With the specter of the Tom Cruise and Katie Holmes three ring circus still fresh in people's minds, the more cynical gossip observers were quick to predict that the relationship would only last as long as the church higher ups could keep from meddling.

Adding to the Scientology intrigue was the fact that Masterson's father reportedly had left the church some years previously for what was being described as actions contradictory to Scientology teachings. Masterson had reportedly cut off all relations with his father and allegedly had not spoken to him in nine years.

But none of that was of any concern to Dakota.

The only thing that was important was that, for the second time in her life, she was in love. And for the time being, it would all be free and easy.

CHAPTER THIRTEEN
SPEED AND SHAKESPEARE

Early in 2013, Dakota was offered the kind of part usually only offered more established actors, a guest shot on the finale of the hit television series *The Office*. It was stunt casting at its funniest as Dakota, one of several interns making their way through the episode, gets to act bewildered and amused at the insanity and laughs generated by the show's regulars. For Dakota, it was a chance to be a part of television history.

And it was also a sign that Hollywood was beginning to move her up the acting hierarchy in an industry where talent often played second fiddle to perception. In the case of Dakota, it was probably a bit of both.

Dakota's next offer came from mainstream Hollywood and from now less a light than Dreamworks Pictures and Steven Spielberg in the form of an all- out action film, *Need for Speed*. The film, based on the popular video game, tells the story of our hero, recently released from prison after being framed for a crime he did not commit by a former business partner, who seeks revenge amid the thrills and chills of a cross country car race. *Need for Speed* had summer blockbuster, overtly commercial written all over it and, on the surface, Dakota's part of the woman torn between allegiance to two men would seem to be little more than eye candy amid the near non- stop thrill ride.

Despite the concern, and a justifiable one in action filmmaking lore, that she would literally be wallpaper amid all the special effects, Dakota immediately found herself in a situation where she was in a giving and human environment. "It's nice to know that I'm in the company of actors who accept what you're offering and give the same right back at you," she related in a promotional interview trailer.

And as paper thin as the set up was, Dakota's Tobey the former girlfriend of the hero who is now dating the villain of the piece, apparently did offer some challenges. While broad based and largely predictable on paper, the consensus was that Dakota's rendering of the classically and emotionally conflicted Tobey was believable and, by turns, sympathetic as defined that by a film that was extremely commercial and obvious but potentially franchise worthy.

"I tried to make her different," she explained in the promo interview trailer. "I didn't see her as stupid and shallow. That's not how I saw her at all. I think it's possible to have a sad character in a race car movie."

Dakota would offer that being in an all-out action film after a career thus far ingrained with primarily small moments, was a lot of fun and it gave her new insights into what it would take for an actress to be noticed in a largely male universe.

Word back from the *Need for Speed* set was that Dakota held her own amid the high speed and car crash film and the consensus among the taste makers of tinsel town was that Dakota would soon be taking the next step up the ladder, the lead in a small but commercial film that would test her ability to open a film to the buying public.

Need for Speed only did passable box office and prospects for a sequel were shaky at best. In a sense that was a good thing for Dakota because actors are typically contractually obligated to do the sequel. The consensus was that there would not be a *Need for Speed 2* and so Dakota was free to try other things.

And it was during her down time that she returned, temporarily, to her modeling roots when she agreed to pose for famed photographer Clairborne Swanson Frank for a book entitled *Young Hollywood*, a series of fashion oriented photos of up and coming Hollywood starlets. Of her photo session at tranquil Virginia Robinson Gardens in Beverly Hills, photographer Frank told the *New York Post,* "She is a gentle spirit. Shooting her was special."

Back in the hunt for her next film, Dakota was not willing to do just any project to land a lead credit. And it was safe to say that she was being offered a lot of those kinds of films. By her standards, the concept had to be intriguing and the character strong to attract her attention and such was definitely the case when she was offered a solid support role in a star laden film called *Cymbeline* (whose title would later be changed to Anarchy).

The film, a modern day reimagining of William Shakespeare's classic tale, had been updated to a modern day relevancy as Sons Of Anarchy meets Romeo and Juliet as a story of corrupt New York City cops and a drug dealing biker gang. The morality play that would be played out in the film featured the likes of Ethan Hawke, Ed Harris, Milla Jovovich, Penn Badgley and Anton Yelchin, in this character driven, rough and tumble scenario.

Dakota plays the character of Imogen the wife of one of the characters who walks a precarious emotional line; offering her the opportunity to dress and play down, wear an uncharacteristic short wig to enhance her defiant stance and, some stills from a scene in which Dakota climbs out of a window dressed in only a tight top and panties, the first worldwide indication of the potential the actress had as a sex symbol in the classic Hollywood mold.

Filming for *Cymbeline* began in mid-August 2013 in New York City. For Dakota, who had long since made The Big Apple her second home, it was an easy commute. Paparazzi would often capture shots of her walking, smiling and at ease and with an occasional wave, to the set. Then it was down to business where Dakota received raves from her fellow cast and filmmakers for her talent and professionalism.

That she was talented and professional had long been a foregone conclusion by the time Dakota did *Cymbeline*. To those in the industry, she was now a legitimate star, bordering on being an A list talent on the verge of full blown celebrity. Like everything else, Dakota took the rave notices and predictions for coming success in stride. She was grateful for being noticed but was determined to not let her press go to her head. Now it was only a matter of biding her time and waiting for that often elusive career defining role.

Filming on the set of *Cymbeline* went smoothly for the first few weeks...

...Interrupted only slightly on the day that it was announced that Dakota had been selected to play Anastasia Steele in *Fifty Shades of Grey*. Her future now seemed assured and up in lights. Only one question remained...

Could she handle it?

CHAPTER FOURTEEN
FEEDING FRENZY

It was all so sudden and dramatic. Dakota had the part of Anastasia in *Fifty Shades of Grey*. She looked out on the rainy New York skyline and cried. She freaked out when the many animals in her apartment would not bother waking from their sleep to congratulate her. But there was only one catch.

She could not tell anybody about it for a while. There was an official announcement that had to be made first, the contract to be agreed to and signed. It was a lot of studio speak but the bottom line was that Dakota spent the next three weeks closed mouthed with the news.

It would be a tough three weeks. Everywhere she went, she most certainly felt that she would either suddenly blurt out the news or that somebody would appear seemingly out of nowhere or offer their congratulations. That she got through the three weeks giving the appearance that everything was normal proved how good an actress she was.

Finally she was free to let the world know.

Once the haters, doubters and just plain anti Dakota Johnson factions lost interest and went away,

Dakota was faced with the expected rush of media interest as she went about her business, completing filming on *Cymbeline*.

And as it had been reported in the *Daily Mail* and *E*, Dakota was making an uncomfortable transition from working actress to the star of the most anticipated film of the decade. Despite being no stranger to the press and publicity, there was an immediate intensity connected to *Fifty Shades of Grey* that was at once off putting. She really had little to say at this point about the film and so she was often shocked and surprised when simple comments were twisted and turned by the tabloids into something exploitive and, at best, marginally true.

It also went without saying that the paparazzi were now swarming like locusts and Dakota, in situations where she had been so far below the radar that she could move freely without being bothered, was now being accosted at every turn. But Dakota would prove to be a quick learner and was soon making her way through this new phase of celebrity with ease.

She said as much in an interview with *Elle*. "I have no idea of how it's all going to go. I plan on handling it gracefully and to live my life as close as I can to how I do now."

Dakota's statement was pretty much in lockstep with those of her stepfather, Banderas, who acknowledged in *The Independent* that Dakota knew enough to take small steps. "She was very happy but very cautious at the same time. And the reason was that she knows that she has a lot of work to do."

However the dye had already been cast. *Cymbeline* had been considered by observers to be a relatively below the radar film but one that would expand Dakota's acting skills. But all of that immediately went by the boards once it was announced that the actress was now officially part of something much bigger. Her *Cymbeline* co-star John Leguizamo recalled when things changed in a conversation that was picked up by countless outlets including *E* and *Entertainmentwise*.

"Here we were doing the movie and she's just Dakota Johnson and the next week it's announced in the trades that she's in *Fifty Shades of Grey* and all of a sudden we're bombarded. But she still remained the same girl even though we had to protect her from the massive amounts of crazy."

The aforementioned 'underwear shot' from *Cymbeline*, which had come and gone in the public consciousness had now been resurrected and transformed into front page news all its own; gossip prognosticators leaping at this as the first sign that the suddenly hot and all out there Dakota did, in fact, have what it took to be the ideal Anastasia in the *Fifty Shades of Grey* movie. It also did not hurt when, shortly after the announcement, Dakota had a staged for the press public meeting with the book's author E.L. James and emerged with the author gushing her approval of the actress for the role.

But while having fun with the inherent glitz and flash of the announcement, Dakota made it plain that, despite the tag of 'mommy porn' that had followed the books from their conception, Dakota, who had diligently read all three volumes of the *Fifty Shades* trilogy, insisted that what she was taking on was serious business.

"I'm not afraid of this story," she told *Entertainment Weekly* prior to the start of filming. "I understand this girl. I get it."

But that would remain a too pat and unsaleable angle for the tabloid press who immediately leaped into the fray with screaming headlines blazing. There was the speculation that Dakota was too nice a girl to pull off the sexually charged requirements in the film. It was not long before her boyfriend, Jordan Masterson, was brought into the mix with several stories with details supplied by the ever-reliable 'unnamed source.' One of the first was that their relationship was already on the rocks because of her taking the role. Another had Jordan insisting that Dakota join Scientology to help her cope with the impending stresses of the film. And depending on which blog you perused, Dakota's parents were either thrilled or aghast at their daughter taking on the role of 'sex slave.'

Yes, the circus had definitely come to town.

Of the later speculation, Dakota's parents were quick to both defend and encourage their daughter's journey into *Fifty Shades*. Her mother Melanie openly defied the Internet haters and stated her daughter was more than up to playing Anastasia. Her father, Don Johnson was equally dismissive of the attacks and took a more pragmatic stance in an interview with *I'm Not Obsessed*.

"This is the family business," he said. "This is what we do. And I am absolutely certain that Dakota will take a piece of material and a character which, for many people, might imagine could be appropriate in some way and turn it into something spectacular."

By this time Dakota seemed to have come to

grips with the spotlight and was able to handle the rush of media interest with ease. When out and about, she was never far from a shouted question or inquiry about the film. Sometimes she would respond with a smile and a bland quip. Sometimes she would just smile and keep right on walking. It also helped that Charlie Hunnam, her co-star in the film, was quite gregarious when dealing with the press, highly quotable, and, consequently, was taking much of the early public relations load off Dakota.

With the completion of *Cymbeline*, Dakota was now free to plunge full bore into preparation for *Fifty Shades of Grey*. Already trim and thin in real life, Dakota, nevertheless, jumped into a regular and rigorous exercise plan with the goal of looking spectacular in and out of clothes. She started a regular exercise program that sometimes included Jordan as her partner. She began a regimen of drinking unfiltered, raw fruit juice. "Obviously I want to look good naked," she laughingly offered in a *Daily Mail/Entertainment Weekly* article.

And as she offered in *Elle*, exercise slowly turned from a necessary chore to a psychological and physical bonus. "I totally understand now why people exercise because it kind of feels fucking awesome."

She also went from her normal blonde locks to a stark and sudden brunette color which was in keeping with the description of Anastasia in the books. It was not surprising that Dakota had done her homework.

All seemed right in Dakota's world. Until three weeks before the film was to begin production in Vancouver, Canada. When, on October 12, Hunnam unexpectedly left the film.

The reasons for the actor's sudden departure were numerous. The more public was that his schedule on his television series *Sons of Anarchy* would not afford the very serious actor the time to truly transition into the Christian Grey character before the start of filming. Another was that the sudden media attention had been too much for the actor. Yet another was that he now felt that the role would not be the best career move. There was also the more sinister speculation that, behind the scenes, there had been ongoing disagreements between actor and director on just how the character of Christian Grey should be portrayed.

The upshot was that the film was suddenly without a star and, while the studio scrambled to regroup, Dakota was suddenly out front and alone to deal with the now even more aggressive media. Speculation instantly cut to the dramatic, if not necessarily true. One story had Dakota so upset about Hunnam leaving that she was also ready to quit. Yet another had the studio so unnerved by the actor's sudden departure that they were going to also let Dakota go and restart their search from scratch.

Through missives on the internet, the studio made it plain that Dakota was still with the film and, reportedly, another screenwriter, Patrick Marber, was being brought in to punch up certain elements of the Kelly Marcel script to feature her character and how secondary characters would interact with her. One thing that remained a constant in this unexpected search for a new Christian Grey was that whoever was chosen would have to have good chemistry with Dakota.

The studio and filmmakers proceeded at light

speed to come up with a new Christian. According to *The Hollywood Reporter*, Universal chairman, Donna Langley, producers Michael DeLuca and Dana Brunetti, director Sam Taylor Johnson and author E.L. James all reportedly submitted lists of four men they would like to see audition for the part of Christian. While nobody was willing to reveal who the names on the list were, the consensus was that two British actors, Jamie Dornan and Christian Cooke, who had been front runners in the first round of auditions but had been passed on when Hunnam had the bigger name, were now considered the prime targets for the Christian Grey casting redeux. That is if they could pass the Dakota test.

Suddenly Dakota's role as actor had morphed into somebody with the power to help guide the future of what the studio had perceived as an all-important franchise. She was regularly brought into meetings with producers to go over an endless amount of actor submissions and to offer her opinion on actors who were now in the running for the role. Producer Michael De Luca made it plain in a conversation with *E News* that the production was not merely paying lip service to Dakota.

"She's just so Anastasia Steele," he said. "She's the best partner a producer could have. She's helping us look through the candidates to see which chemistry kind of captures our attention."

Dakota was doing more than checking out pictures and offering initial impressions. As the cut down date neared for the selection of a new Christian Grey, the actress was once again meeting with the finalists in stealth rehearsals to see if the chemistry she had with Hunamm could be duplicated. The only difference being that the actors now had to prove they were a match for Dakota.

At a Hollywood awards presentation, film co-producer Michael DeLuca spent much of the evening fielding questions about the state of *Fifty Shades of Grey* and, in particular, how Dakota was holding up under the pressure of this unexpected turn of events. DeLuca told the *Los Angeles Times* that night that Dakota was fine, anxious to get on the set and that he was confident that Dakota could play Anastasia no matter who ended up playing Christian Grey.

"I happen to think that Dakota could have chemistry with a mailbox," the producer chuckled. "But we're going to help her out and hook her up with the right person."

On October 24, 2013, it was announced that Jamie Dornan was the new Christian Grey.

Dornan had submitted an on-tape audition for the first rounding of casting for Grey but did not take it too hard when he had not progressed to an actual meeting with Dakota and the director. In fact he was the picture of quiet confidence in his London home as he contemplated the birth of his first child and a slate of upcoming television work. But that changed one night when a round of late night television viewing was interrupted by a phone call from the states. Hunnam had dropped out of the role of Christian Grey and could he be on a flight to Los Angeles as soon as possible.

Dakota was more than a touch weary at the on-going drama connected to the film and was equal parts enthusiastic and nervous at the process of having to go through yet another audition with Dornan. Dornan's audition with Dakota would be a two-part test, the first being the interview scene that set the stage for Christian and Anastasia's relationship and the second was the climactic sequence that plays out at the end of the book. The chemistry between the pair was immediate with Dakota marveling at how Dornan could move between the softer and more aggressive sides of Grey's personality with relative ease. Dakota was also quick to note that Dornan had classic good looks.

"Ultimately the decision that was made was great," Dakota offered to *The Straits Times*. "Jamie's wonderful."

Once again Dornan, with his brooding good looks and an extensive background, given his relatively young age, in acting, modeling and music, seemed the ideal choice. An important point being that he came out publically saying that he was totally committed to the role and the films. To drive that point home to an increasingly anxious fan base, the screen couple would have their official unveiling in a mid-November photo and interview cover driven piece in *Entertainment Weekly*. For her part, Dakota seemed confident and self-assured in talking up the behind the scenes of her casting and her ongoing preparation for the film. Everything seemed a go.

With some last minute changes.

Initially *Fifty Shades* had been set to go before the cameras in early November for an August 2014 release. With the scramble to replace Hunamm, the date to begin filming had been bumped up to late November. Finally it was revealed that while the

December 1st start date would remain intact, the release date of the first in the *Fifty Shades* film trilogy had now been pushed back to a Valentines' Day 2015 unveiling. There were the inevitable rumors and speculation.

Many thought the extra time would allow for any unexpected problems that might arise. Others speculated that, as a cost cutting measure by the always economically inclined studio, a plan was a foot to shoot all three films back to back to back. There was also speculation that the extra-long production would allow the company to film two different versions of the film, one rated R for general audiences who might not be familiar with the books and the always daring NC-17 for the hardcore fans of the books who wanted to see everything they had read up on the screen.

One thing was certain. Amid all the hype and speculation Dakota made it very plain that her foray into the world of *Fifty Shades of Grey* would not be chaperoned by her family.

"I'm obviously not going to let them (her parents) take part in this experience," she told *Entertainment Weekly*. "I don't need to watch movies of them where they do things like this. Why would you want them to do that with me?"

Producer Dana Brunetti officially opened the filming of *Fifty Shades of Grey* when he tweeted a picture of a film slate, indicating the title of the film and the first day and scene number. Underneath the photo was the simple caption, 'Here we go.'

The first official day of film commenced on the dot of December 1st, under the code name The

Adventures Of Max and Banks to throw off a possible deluge of *Fifty Shades* fans descending upon the production, with a seemingly nondescript scene with Dakota and her co -star Jamie Dornan having tea at an outdoor café. The crude stills taken from behind the camera were telling. Even in this simple scene, the actress was shy, sultry and just a bit curious about this man, Christian Grey, who had suddenly entered her life.

Those first days were filled with high expectations and no small amount of excitement. No moment, no matter how small or insignificant, was above being newsworthy as the media instantly ran wild with blaring headlines for even the most un newsworthy event.

Whatever scenario would ultimately play out remained to be seen. But one thing was for certain. By early December, Dakota was already on the ground in Vancouver, Canada...

Slipping into the skin of Anastasia Steele.

CHAPTER FIFTEEN
DAKOTA DIGS DEEP

It's cold in Vancouver in December. In the storyline of *Fifty Shades of Grey* it is supposed to be a bright, sunny day. During one of the early days on set, Dakota was dressing for both the fantasy and the reality.

Dakota showed up on set in a heavy overcoat and boots against the cold. But that did not prevent the actress from being immediately identified. Hardcore fans had quickly cut through the code names and fuzzy information and, on this particular day, had tracked down the *Fifty Shades* production on a busy street of hip shops, restaurants and boutiques.

Film crews on the streets of Vancouver, Canada had long ago stopped being the object of curiosity. With Canada's liberal working policies and generous budget and tax regulations, the land across the upper US border had quickly become Hollywood North. But those privy to those first days of shooting on Fifty Shades of Grey, could sense something different in the air.

There was a sense of positive tension and excitement as crew members positioned lights and cameras. Director Johnson was known for running a straightforward but creatively loose set and as she wandered around, checking with her lighting people, discussing the upcoming scenes with her director of photography and talking easily with her actors, there were sure signs that, in Johnson's creative view the movie was on a steady course. The consensus was that *Fifty Shades of Grey* had to be one of the biggest projects in the history of film but, early on, it seemed like nobody connected to the film had a care in the world.

But early on in the process, Dakota would admit to *Vanity Fair* that the suddenly universal importance of this film in millions of people's minds had given her some uneasy moments. She was also quick to point out that, only a few days into filming, it had been an easy ride.

"It's been a very smooth, fun and creative experience," she offered. "I think going into something like this you kind of have these different fears of what it could be like and none of those things are happening. We all get along real well, the crew is amazing and we're all just trying to make this project the best it can be."

But all the happy talk in the world could not dissuade Dakota from feeling some heat. While those who had greeted Dakota's casting with negative attacks, had seemingly faded into the background. However actor Victor Rasuk, recalled to *Watch Magazine* that during his days on the *Fifty Shades of Grey* set and, especially in his scenes with Dakota, there was still quite a bit of tension in the air. "When I first got the role and was working with Dakota, there were definitely a lot of haters out there. But by the time I did my scenes with Dakota, I knew I had been working with a fantastic actress."

During a lengthy wait before the first shot of the day, Dakota smiled and waved to fans who were thrilled at the response. Sometime later, Dakota now stripped to an enticing school girl short skirt and blouse, was seen exuding sexuality as she walked through a scene and, in a sequence in which she looked into the window of an open car, libidos received an early shot to what Anastasia was all about in the skirt rising tightly to show the outline of much toned legs and posterior.

If there was any hint of nervousness during the early days of filming, Dakota was hiding it well. She was all smiles and self- deprecating humor as she wandered in and out of makeup and wardrobe rooms. Even in these early scenes, in which she is looking more school girl and dressed down, there was a sense of sly, sexy glamour about her. It did not come as a surprise to those who had been up close and personal with the actress since she started in the business. The Dakota during those first days of filming on *Fifty Shades of Grey* was pretty much the Dakota everybody had always known. She continued to remain bright, fresh and unfazed by it all.

But the tension was reportedly palpable on the set during some sequences in which Anastasia and Christian are in a meeting in which Christian lays his cards on the table about his bondage and sadomasochistic tastes and a need for total control in their relationship. And yes, that day also produced a first kiss between the couple, albeit a sedate peck on Christian' cheek by Anastasia.

But when it came to the diehard fans who were living by every rumor, scrap of information and the few leaked photos, it was the kiss literally seen around the world. Web sites around the world put up the furtive photos that had been taken and blared out that this was indeed the beginning of the most anticipated film relationship of all time. These early reports were, admittedly, colored by tabloid and gossip speculation and breathless prose but the point was being made. There for the world to see were Anastasia and Christian and they were truly together.

Dakota was no stranger to the reality of a film set, the long, often boring hours between moments of actual filming and adjusted easily to the by now familiar nuts and bolts of filmmaking. She was often found standing patiently while the camera man adjusted an angle or perspective that would feature her. To keep her energy up, she was reportedly drinking quantities of specially ordered juice from a nearby restaurant.

Although films are generally shot in bits and pieces and, often, out of order, during those early days there seemed to be some rhyme or reason, especially when it came to establishing Anastasia and Christian's relationship. Early shots involving Dakota acknowledged Grey's business empire and, in a sequence that immediately set the internet twittering, Dakota and Jamie are seen leaving his office building. He looking tight lipped and impassive and she appearing distracted and uncertain. In her hand was clutched a plain, brown envelope. Those privy to the specifics of the *Fifty Shades* universe instantly speculated that the envelope contained the infamous contract that Anastasia would sign and thus be plunged into Christian's world of dominance and submission.

Those early days of filming allowed some moments of relaxation for Dakota. Although Dakota had made it plain that she did not want her parents on the set, her half -sister, Stella, was apparently on Dakota's guest list. The 17 year-old was spotted on several occasions, observing her sister filming and chatting easily with cast and crewmembers.

Conspicuous by his at least public absence from the set was Dakota's boyfriend Jordan. The tabloid press had switched into high gear on that front as the production came closer to starting up. Reportedly, Jordan was feeling uneasy about Dakota's doing the movie and that her doing the sexually charged films might threaten their relationship. There were also reports that Jordan had been pushing for Dakota to convert to Scientology in an attempt to deal with the public and private pressures that would most certainly come with her doing the film. All of which was given credence by the fact that the last time Dakota and Jordan had been photographed together had been two months before the start of production. The real reason Jordan was not seen early on in the shoot was anybody's guess.

As part of the 'silly season' of reporting that surrounded the *Fifty Shades of Grey* production, a hilarious but marginally believable story was floated that the extremely sexual nature of the film would be the ultimate death to any cast member's relationship. The speculation pointed to *Fifty Shades* actress Rita Ora who had reportedly broken up with her DJ boyfriend Calvin Harris during the production of the film as well as Dakota's eternally shaky relationship with Jordan. What the story failed to mention was the fact that Dakota's co-star Jamie, recently married and more recently the father of a baby daughter, was quite happy and settled in his personal life.

However Jordan's absence would burn bright well beyond this fleeting 'cursed film' story when *Showbiz Spy* and *The National Enquirer* breathlessly reported that Dakota's former secret beau, Stephen Dorff, was allegedly making a new round of advances toward Dakota. Dakota had nothing to say on the subject but her parents certainly did. Both Don Johnson and Melanie Griffith reportedly made it very plain in a *Showbiz Spy* story that they did not want Dorff anywhere near their daughter.

The first full week of filming was a bit scattershot. With the arrival of actress Eloise Mumford, who plays Anastasia's roommate Kate. Dakota and Eloise were slated to shoot a handful of scenes surrounding the storyline in which Anastasia replaces Kate for the interview with Christian that starts it all. Otherwise Dakota was largely missing from public view in the days leading up to Christmas. This was due, in large part, to the fact that Jamie Dornan's wife, Amelia Warner, had just given birth to the couple's first child, a baby girl, and the actor had been given a couple of days off to bond with his newly expanded family.

Dornan was back a couple of days later and was immediately thrust into the middle of a tense bit of storyline in which Christian attends Anastasia's graduation and meets her parents for the first time. Dakota moved her character believably into the moment with photos from the set indicating her character alternately uneasy, distracted and finally upbeat at this pivotal moment in the storyline.

Then it was on to some sequences in which Christian and Anastasia walking down the street, all smiles, closeness and the occasional kiss; all signs that at least at this point the relationship, kinks and all, seems to be working. The on-camera chemistry was obvious as witness another sequence in which Dakota and Jamie broke into a bit of up close and personal ballroom dancing on a city street, to reflect the fact that the two actors were, indeed, getting along and that all the action in *Fifty Shades* would not be strictly sexual.

The plot would definitely thicken the following day when the scenes were filmed in which Christian saves Anastasia from being hit by a bike. In the moments after the near miss the couple looked lovingly, yes lovingly, into each other's eyes as they held each other tight. Dakota, looking doe eyed and vulnerable and Jamie with a soft, less stern expression was a definite clue that the film version of *Fifty Shades of Grey*, might well turn out to be less about domination and more about romance.

But as filming progressed, *Fifty Shades of Grey* exposed a potential problem in Dakota. The actress was the quintessential nice person who would stop and talk to crew members, security, fans, just about anybody who happened to cross her path. On the surface that did not appear to be a problem. But the cast and crew soon began to notice that when Dakota was too preoccupied in being nice, she tended to become distracted from the filmmaking business at hand.

On the other hand, Jamie, who was prone to wanting to be left alone when he was not working, was one of the first to notice Dakota's niceness and took it upon himself to intercede when he sensed she was getting in over her head. It was reported on several occasions that Jamie would walk over to Dakota and politely tell the person she was talking to that she needed to be left alone. That Jamie might be bordering on overprotective or just playing out an extension of his character was never discussed.

When not filming, Dakota would regularly take advantage of Vancouver's high-end shopping and fashion scene. She would often be spotted walking down a street with bags and bundles in her arms and was reportedly dropping as much as $1500 on such luxuries as fashionable shoes. And despite the persistent rumors of trouble in her relationship with Jordan, the couple were suddenly spotted together again on several occasions walking the streets of Vancouver. If their body language was any indication, any trouble between them, not surprisingly, appeared to be in the imagination of the tabloid reporters.

The *Fifty Shades Of Grey* production took a few days off with the Christmas holidays approaching and, despite the continued rumors of discord between Dakota and Justin because of the sex scenes in the film, she was spotted happy and arm in arm with her beau on a fun filled family reunion on the slopes of Aspen, Colorado with her mother and extended family.

But those rumors of trouble in paradise would not go away and, in fact, persisted in high gear when, according to *Digital Journal*, the *Fifty Shades of Grey* company left Vancouver, due partially to a run of bad weather in Canada for Tenerife in the Canary Islands to finally begin filming the more erotically charged scenes, in this case the much ballyhooed honeymoon sequence and then on to Madrid to shoot some scenes centered around Christian's business side.

Observers of the film's progress were certainly relishing this portion of the shoot. The so called 'dirty bits' were the overriding reason people had bought the original books and how true the movie would be to the book's erotic moments might well spell success or failure. Following the completion of the film, Dakota would talk about the reality of shooting the hoped for hot sex with *Today*.

"It's not like a romantic situation," she explained. "It was more like technical and choreographed. It was like more of a task."

Dakota acknowledged that the fact that Jamie and her got along so well was a key to making the erotic moments believable. "That was a big part of it, having that trust. Because we got ourselves into situations that didn't feel that sort of natural and they're not that easy, you need to have that trust."

But even when things seemed to be going well on the *Fifty Shades of Grey* set, the tabloid press was working overtime to create sensation and controversy. And so the latest bombshell always seemed to be right around the corner.

It was announced early in January by the producers that what was originally going to be the trilogy of movies based on the three books was now being condensed into one and only one movie. And that some of the scenes to be filmed on the Canary Islands location were actually scenes from the third book that would be part of the condensing process. The early response from the fans was decidedly negative.

Rumors began to circulate. It was the usual stuff. The film was already wildly over budget and behind schedule. The director and producers were at odds about the direction the film should take. The dailies had not been that great. And of course that time honored Hollywood saw, the actors had begun to show their true colors and were suddenly not up to the task. A much more economically driven speculation was that it had suddenly been determined that a Fifty Shades movie or movies would be playing to the choir and that a loyal fan base alone might not ultimately be enough to justify three separate films over a number of years.

The speculation ran through the blogosphere so fast that film company Universal was literally dragged into making a statement to the effect that the company had every intention of making all three movies but that sequels beyond the first film would depend on how well the first film did at the box office.

Once again, at this point, for better or worse, Dakota and the rest of the filmmakers were in the middle of another controversy. All they could do was continue to work.

Given the high profile nature of the project, the production of *Fifty Shades* was conspicuous by the fact that there was more rumor and gossip swirling around Dakota than any actual facts. That may well have been because Dakota, running true to form, was keeping a low key, nose to the grindstone professional profile in and around the movie.

However, as *Fifty Shades of Grey* moved into the proverbial home stretch of filming, there was a slight turn in perception. The more outlandish rumors and tabloid mongering had suddenly become the front page story. By contrast, the often routine and yes occasionally boring set reports were regulated to small print and sidebar status. And of course there were elements of the anti-*Fifty Shades of Grey* backlash against author James for her alleged lack of writing talent, the countless millions she had made and the continued question of her seeming inability to put out another book since the *Fifty Shades* trilogy that had never been far from the coverage of the film. There was little the production company could do in the face of this onslaught but deny all charges and put the best possible spin out in response, knowing all the while that all would be forgotten and forgiven if the movie was good.

As *Fifty Shades of Grey* moved into the new year, there was some doubt among media observers as to whether Dakota had hitched her career to a rocket to the stars or a Titanic. For her part, Dakota could not be bothered. She was too busy doing what actors do. Which was her best.

CHAPTER SIXTEEN
GOOD TIMES, BAD TIMES

But by 2013, the last thing on Dakota's mind was whether *Fifty Shades of Grey* would make her career or destroy it. It was Christmas and she was already onto other things.

Fifty Shades of Grey was now in the final laps of a month's long home stretch and the consensus from those privy to the production was that Dakota had given a first rate performance of the very difficult and demanding material. And according to the buzz being generated surrounding the film, Dakota would emerge from the film as a legitimate star.

Worthy of the star-making machinery that was already being set in motion.

Offers for the prized cover of many top level magazines were being considered and the first to strike gold would be *Elle* with an extensive interview and a sizzling cover and inside photo spread with Dakota playing *Fifty Shades* with a series of erotically charged poses. The interview used her *Fifty Shades'* success as a jumping off point for a solid character driven look into Dakota's life and the road to success. But it would not be all work and no play during the holidays.

Dakota's shaky relationship with Jordan now appeared, for the moment, to be on sturdier ground. During the photo shoot for *Elle*, she made a point of fielding a call from him and saying the Jordan had gotten her the perfect Christmas gift. A sink.

Fifty Shades of Grey wrapped on February 23, 2014. The announcement became official when E.L. James, who had been a frequent visitor to the production, unleashed an Instagram of herself and director Johnson holding up glasses of what were presumably champagne. Under the photo was the caption That's a wrap.

The film's producers did not waste any time getting the publicity ball rolling. At March's Las Vegas Cinema Con, the first footage of the film was leaked. The response was decidedly mixed. Many came away disappointed that the first look at *Fifty Shades* the movie seemed to focus more on the love story between Christian and Anastasia and less on the couple's erotic adventures. This, in turn, gave rise to the fear that the movie would not live up to the book. Word quickly got out that the first response to the footage had been mixed and everybody connected to the movie did their best to put a positive spin on things.

Dakota was in Singapore for Fashion Week when she was approached for comment and, as reported in countless media outlets, she put up a spirited defense. "Everything is a little secret but I can tell you that I think people will be pleased with the movie. I'm doing the movie because I love it and I believe in the story and I believe in the books and I hope that I will do them justice."

Dakota was in a euphoric state at the conclusion

of the filming. She felt in her creative gut that she had given an outstanding performance and was excited at the prospects for the future. Understandably she took some time off. But it seemed like almost immediately she was up for the next thing.

Hollywood studios were quick to take notice of the growing perception of Dakota as the new 'It' girl. A rush of substantial parts in high profile studio projects was soon piling up at her doorstep and, in the time honored tradition of striking while the iron is hot, Dakota was soon filling out her work card with several projects for the remainder of 2014.

To the degree that she appeared in a short film entitled *Closed Set*. All that is known about this truly obscure item was that it was directed by veteran cinematographer Mitchell Amundsen , that Dakota's character was known simply as The Leading Lady and that it was made largely as a quasi- industrial film to showcase a film sensor/image enhancer called the 6K Red Dragon. What is known about this obscurity that it has been seen sporadically at industry conventions and exhibitions.

By March Dakota was in serious negotiation to star opposite Johnny Depp in *Black Mass*, the film biography of Irish mobster Whitey Bulger. The deal was struck in April and by May she was on the east coast in the guise of Lindsey Cyr, the girlfriend of Bulger and the mother of his child. Playing in the same picture and in the same scenes as Depp had Dakota in a fierce awestruck state but she quickly got beyond the hero worship stage and, according to reports, turned in another first rate performance. It was then that she felt safe in returning to Dakota fan girl.

"It was one of the best experiences of my life so far," she told *Vogue*

And *Black Mass* would seemingly be the final nail in the coffin of her relationship with Jordan. While Jordan had reportedly visited Dakota on the set of *Black Mass*, it was also reported in the tabloid press that Dakota had been secretly involved with her fellow *Black Mass* castmate Benedict Cumerbatch. In typical tabloid manner, that rumor had the shelf life of about a day.

As with just about everything in her personal life, the final break up was done so below the radar that it would take until July when a chance paparazzi shot of Dakota walking down a New York street in a romantic clinch with Matthew Hitt, a member of the band Drowners revealed Dakota's new beau to the world. That no follow up stories seemed eminent, it put this latest report in doubt or maybe Dakota sensed the press intrusion building and just took the alleged relationship underground.

Media interest in her new beau was immediate and detailed. He was a model as well as a musician. He had a college degree in English Literature and was born in Wales. Creative, intellectual and good looking. Hitt fit Dakota's criterion to a T.

But there was an equally vocal opinion that a relationship with Matthew was simply a publicity stunt to draw attention to *Fifty Shades* and that the fact that Jamie was publically and happily married was the only thing that kept the gossip mongers from fabricating a Dakota/Jamie romance to goose interest.

Unlike most models, who forsake their fashion roots once they make the transition to acting, Dakota had, through occasional photo shoots and good friends within the fashion industry, managed to maintain strong ties with the fashion industry. During a July holiday in Europe, Dakota would reestablish her fashion sense in a variety of informal appearances. At the annual Glastonbury Music Festival, the actress was spotted walking hand in hand with fashion designer Stella McCartney (the daughter of Paul McCartney). At the prestigious Met Festival she was the guest of top fashion designer Jason Wu and paraded down the red carpet dressed in a dazzling Wu dress. She would also be an honored guest at the Chantel Haute Couture show in Paris.

Dakota's notoriety had quickly seeped into her parent's lives as well. Neither Johnson nor Griffith, who were also active in their own professional lives, could get very far into promoting their own current project without having to talk about their daughter. Both took the questions with grace and were effusive in their encouragement of Dakota. A perfect example being when Johnson was on the stump for his latest film *Cold In July* and the inevitable Dakota questions came up in an excerpt covered by *Total Film* and numerous other outlets.

"I'm exceedingly proud of my daughter," he said. "She's a gifted actress. I don't speak about the obvious salacious nonsense. We all take on challenges. For Dakota this is just another part of what I think will be a long and important career."

Late in July brought the first salvo from *Fifty Shades of Grey* marketing department in the form of the very first trailer for the film that, at the time, was undergoing an extensive final edit. The tension packed trailer showed scattered glimpses of the controversial sex play and was expertly cut to maximize tension and anticipation for the coming film. The trailer went viral and was immediately seen by millions and would ultimately become the most viewed trailer of 2014.

Dakota was thrilled with the trailer but then, with a little time to deal with her feelings, suddenly decided that she was a little embarrassed as well. At which point she rang up her parents and laid down the law that she did not want them to see the movie. "I think I would love to have my parents experience it with me," she offered in a *National Ledger* article. "But I can't really do that because of what it entails. I talk to them about problems with my landlords. That's my talking point with my family."

Johnson and Griffith readily agreed with Griffith explaining the situation to *Indiewire*. "I have not seen the movie. I don't think I'm going to see it. Dakota said 'You guys cannot come. There's no way.' So we're not going."

Many of the scripts being offered Dakota were, in a sense, the obvious ones, parts in big budget, commercial outings that would bring a lot of money. But true to form, Dakota continued to think with her creative soul rather than her bank account and so, despite *Black Mass* being assured of a big studio release on thousands of screens, she was deliberately choosing smaller, more character driven films in an attempt to showcase her skills as a legitimate actress.

Dakota knew the reality of her burgeoning career. Whether she liked it or not, she would forever be tied to *Fifty Shades of Grey* and its follow up films. But while grateful for this immense, career making opportunity, she was bound and determined to forge a widely divergent career of which *Fifty Shades* would hopefully be only a footnote.

Which was why her first film following *Black Mass* was a much smaller and more character driven piece called *A Bigger Splash*. *A Bigger Splash*, based on the 1969 French crime drama *La Piscine*, was exactly what she was looking for, a taught, tense and very European in tone story of a couple on holiday who form an unusual relationship with a girl that ultimately leads to a sinister ending. Dakota was immediately thrilled with the idea of working alongside two veteran actors, Ralph Fiennes and Tilda Swinton. That the film would be filming in Italy was the literal icing on the cake. By August, Dakota was once again before the camera. And as time permitted, she would attend several galas in the literal center of fashion and do a photo shoot that showcased Dakota in lighter tones far removed from her *Fifty Shades* starkness.

Further spreading her wings, Dakota also added the title producer to her resume when she agreed to produce and star in *Forever Interrupted*, based on the novel by Taylor Jenkins Reid. This small but poignant tale focuses on a woman who elopes after a whirlwind romance. In the aftermath of the tragic death of her husband, the woman forms an uneasy relationship with her dead lover's mother. These are the kinds of projects that often wind up in development hell unless a star of some notoriety agrees to do it. It went without question that those connected to *Forever Interrupted* were beside themselves when Dakota signed on.

Producer Nathan Kahane told *Up and Comers,*

'We're thrilled that Dakota has come on board, not only starring but taking an active role behind the camera." Author Reid was likewise happy, telling *USA Today* that Dakota was the perfect choice. "I don't think Dakota will need much help from me in figuring out the role. She's a great actress with such innate likeability."

More *Forever Interrupted* praise would come from producer Amy Baer who told *Virgin Media,* "Dakota will be exquisite as Elsie who has to deal with the sudden loss of a great love. She is a deeply thoughtful, sensitive and smart woman and actress."

Dakota's seemingly intelligent career choices came as a surprise to veteran observers of the film industry who had witnessed many performers 'cashing in' at the first sign of success. Not so surprised was Dakota's mother, Melanie, who, as reported in *Dakota Johnson Life*, was effusive in how well her daughter's career was progressing.

"I think Dakota is going to be better than me and better than my mom," she proclaimed at the Locarno Film Festival. "She has learned from all the mistakes I've made and all of the things that have happened to my mom. She is just a force of nature and she is a very good actress."

Praise from father Don was also front and center in an interview with *USA Today*. "She is a very independent little girl. She was adamant about doing her career on her own without any assistance. She's gifted and painfully honest with people who aren't prepared for it."

Into August, Dakota appeared in a state of grace. Professionally she was busy and fulfilled. Personally she seemed content and while the relationship question would continue to be a tabloid topic, the actress managed to keep her private life a question mark. The pre-release hype on *Fifty Shades of Grey* was stepping into high gear with more and more of her time, some six months before the release of the film, being devoted to doing press for the film. And now that Jamie was finished with his first post *Fifty Shades* project, they would often do interviews together.

And in those instances the ease that had marked their work on the film was apparent as they sat on TV talk show couches and fielded largely softball questions from the press. Dakota proved particularly deft at deflecting questions she was under orders not to talk about in great depth and turning almost all the questions into something of a joking quip.

The actress must have sensed that, this being a visual journalistic world, that essentially showing up and letting the cameras project her image to the world was enough. And with the blogosphere being what it was, just about anything she said, no matter how trivial, would be picked up by endless websites and blasted around the world. One would occasionally get the impression that Dakota would rather be doing something else. But the reality was that Dakota had quickly evolved into the consummate professional.

Which would lead into even more media speculation. Stories began to appear that indicated the actress, already weary of the hype of *Fifty Shades of Grey*, was, professionally and personally, doing everything possible to distance herself from her upcoming breakthrough film. Taking what many consider more serious roles and, reportedly, even changing boyfriends in order to cultivate a less controversial resume and to be taken as a serious actress. It all seemed a bit farfetched and a thinly veiled grasp at creating headlines where, going into September, there really wasn't much to talk about except the endless recycling of old *Fifty Shades* news and quotes. In that sense, Dakota may well have already made her point.

CHAPTER SEVENTEEN
COUNTDOWN...

If Dakota had any idea that she was about to witness yet another divorce very close to home, she was keeping it to herself. But the reality was that about the time she was filming A *Bigger Splash* in Italy, it was announced that Antonio Banderas and her mother Melanie had filed for divorce after 18 years of marriage. In fact, if press reports were to be believed, Dakota had absolutely zero to say about her mother's fourth divorce.

Perhaps with good reason.

Dakota had grown up around marriages, divorces and the resultant blended families. She had her own relationships that ultimately dissolved. In a very real sense, the idea of people not staying together forever had become part of her emotional template, to be considered but then ultimately put on the back burner as life went on. Dakota was not dead to the process and, most certainly, felt a degree of sadness. But it was just not something to be obsessed over. And so life went on.

And into the inevitable 'silly season' of Dakota rumors and gossip. Depending on what people read or even remotely believed, the actress was either dead, married, pregnant, the highest paid model in the world and in talks to play the next 'Bond Girl.' But easily the most outlandish speculation was that Dakota was in serious consideration to be named *Time* Magazine's Person Of The Year.

On a more serious note...

...In August, the Hollywood trade publication *Variety* gave its official stamp on Dakota as a comer in the industry when she was named one of the 10 stars to watch in 2014. Unlike some of the more laughable top ten lists put together by the fan magazines, *Variety's* offering served as a guide to the decision makers in Hollywood. In the case of Dakota, the dye had been cast. She seemed fully capable of opening a studio picture (although in the case of *Fifty Shades of Grey* it remained to be seen) and had proven a solid support/character actress and, if *Variety* was correct, would be working a lot in the coming years.

Not that Dakota was letting honors like this go to her head. On the set of *A Bigger Splash* she was reportedly the consummate professional. Her scenes with the much more experienced Fiennes and Swinton reportedly showcased the actress as mature beyond her years, one who reportedly could play mysterious, conniving and moments of tension and dark intent. It was a time of real growth after a trial by fire in which she was the center of attention in the movie version of a pop culture success story. In *A Bigger Splash*, she could quite simply just do the work.

But no matter how seemingly prestigious or artful her post *Fifty Shades of Grey* work was shaping up to be, the specter of Anastasia Steele was never too far behind. And in late August, *The Hollywood Reporter* dropped a bit of a bombshell when, during an interview with legendary actress and Dakota's grandmother Tippi Hedren, she offered that the much reported family support for Dakota in *Fifty Shades* might be a smokescreen for some discontent.

"I understand Don Johnson is very upset about her being in the film," she revealed. "He kind of had the same feeling that I do. I've seen the trailer and that's all I have to watch."

That it was *The Hollywood Reporter* who reported Hedren's comments and that she made no immediate comments to the effect that she had been misquoted or taken out of context was added validity to the fact that Dakota's father was not thrilled with his daughter's upcoming appearance in the *Fifty Shades of Grey* movie.

Not surprisingly it was Dakota's mother, Melanie, who, in *The Express*, continued to be in her daughter's corner, reportedly stating that it was sad that the rest of the family did not support Dakota's choice and that Dakota had every right to take a role that would most certainly advance her career.

There was no immediate response from Dakota to her grandmother's comments but it was a safe bet that some telephone conversations were exchanged between Dakota and her family. In fact Dakota into September had seemingly dropped off the hard or even soft news radar. It was a given that she was working but no reports were forthcoming from film sets. There were the occasional paparazzi shots of the actress with friends or at some event but, otherwise, Dakota Johnson was suddenly invisible to the world at large.

Except when she decided to do a good deed. While in Italy, she was informed of the plight of a rancher who, owing to economic hard times, was going to have to destroy eight of his horses. Dakota immediately donated a total of $8,000 for the upkeep of the horses, a sure sign that Dakota had heart as well as talent.

It was a slippery slope for Dakota. The actress continued to toe a traditional career line, to do good work in the most challenging projects. It was the press, however, that continued to blare out the headlines that Dakota was indeed Hollywood royalty. When she did talk, Dakota continued to express a desire to run from such accolades.

Which, most certainly, was the way she wanted it. She had learned well the up side and down side of constantly being in the public eye. Not enough exposure and one became a non-entity on the Hollywood radar. Too much exposure and one became Lindsay Lohan and Justin Bieber. Dakota had, in a sense become an old school kind of working actress. She had already proven with the early round of promotion on *Fifty Shades of Grey* that she would willingly do everything she could to promote her work. But she was not one to linger too long. Once the purposeful work was done, Dakota was easily slipping back into as normal a life as possible until the next call came her way.

"Everybody has an opinion about living in the public eye," she told *Variety*. "In a good way it's made me a lot stronger and more resilient."

Which meant having a personal life away from the world. After the initial photos of Matthew Hitt and herself hit the Internet, the couple, for paparazzi and tabloid purposes, had seemed to disappear; proving that it was possible to have a life away from prying eyes.

Six months before the official release of *Fifty Shades of Grey*, Dakota was in a state of personal and professional grace. But when it came time for the final push for *Fifty Shades* and it was time for her to jump…

…Dakota would be the first to say how high.

CHAPTER EIGHTEEN
...TO FIFTY SHADES

Midway through September, *Cymbeline* was making its way through the festival circuit in search of rave reviews and a distribution deal. Early reviews for the film were decidedly mixed with reviewers agreeing on the fact that trying to update Shakespeare in a modern setting had proven awkward. But those same reviewers were fairly generous if curt in their opinion of Dakota's work in the film with a review on *Playlist* saying that Dakota's performance was "pretty decent."

And although it was reported with its tongue planted firmly in its journalistic cheek, the *Daily Mail* set tongues a wagging in September with a report that the latest member of the Kardashian clan, Kendall Jenner, was using her brand rather than any innate talent to get a role in the second *Fifty Shades of Grey* movie. Of particular note was the fact that the tabloids cooked the story to indicate that Jenner was after Dakota's role. That notion immediately put the story in doubt. Because for better or worse, Dakota and Anastasia were connected for all time and it did not appear that anybody was going to wrestle the role away from her.

Although it was noted not long after the completion of *Fifty Shades of Grey* that Dakota, running contrary to the notion that actors working in potential franchises must agree to sequels, had not been formally signed to the second film in the trilogy. While no actual figure was ever quoted as to how much Dakota was getting for the first film, reports surfaced that she was getting $125,000, as was her co-star (stories further down the road would speculate that both stars were actually getting a million plus). It was likely that her participation in the rest of the series would jack up her asking price quite substantially and that Dakota returning was assured.

As befitting the new 'it' girl, a big part of the Dakota daily news cycle seemed to center around a seemingly never ending series of projects that the actress was in various stages of negotiation for. The notion was floated that Dakota was inclined to return to series television which, which considering her status in films, seemed more a flight of fantasy. More logical was the idea that Dakota was ready to test herself on the Broadway stage but, given her current slate of film projects, would be chalked up to far in the future. Easily the most enticing and continuing bit of speculation was that the actress was being considered for the next Bond Girl.

It was a lot of speculation to deal with and Dakota dealt with it by ignoring it. Throughout the summer, she remained the consummate working actress in Italy, hoping for the best for *Cymbeline's* eminent release and gearing up for the stretch run of promotion for *Fifty Shades of Grey* that was right around the corner. In fact the growing mania for the upcoming film was so great that *Vogue Magazine*, some six months before the release of the film, had already announced that their February 2015 issue would have a *Fifty Shades of Grey* cover.

And the studio was doing its due diligence in fanning the flames for all things *Fifty Shades*. Besides the initial trailer, stills from the film as well as promotional photos were being leaked to the media at various intervals. In one hilarious shot, the director, holding what appears to be a riding crop, is standing menacingly over wide eyed Dakota and Jamie. Dakota was also center stage in a still from the movie in which Anastasia is seen provocatively chewing on a pencil emblazoned with Christian's corporate logo.

But while Dakota was doing everything that was asked of her in terms of promoting *Fifty Shades of Grey*, she was also pulling away from the film that, in mere months, would forever mark her in the eyes of the world. During an appearance at a London fashion show for designer pal Stella McCartney, Dakota amazed onlookers as she strode the red carpet and show proper with blonde hair while dressed in an all - white dress. It was a striking image, far removed from that of Anastasia, and one that reinforced the notion that Dakota was an actress who could turn her looks around on a dime. As witness the fact that, by the time Dakota had returned to New York late in September, she was once again a Brunette.

Within the week, Dakota was touching down in Los Angeles, still a brunette, on a flight that also had Jamie on the passenger manifesto. They made a bit of a show for the paparazzi as they exited the plane separately. The reality of their appearance, and not an uncommon one in the film industry, was that some reshoots had been required on *Fifty Shades of Grey* and Dakota and Jamie were in LA and finally back to Vancouver for that purpose. The reshoots, according to *Fashion Times*, were shot in a stealth manner, reportedly sequences involving other actors as well. The reshoots, in and of themselves, were not so much a concern as was the rabid media speculation surrounding them.

There was the gossip and tabloid reports that the reshoots were required for the unrated version of the film even though it had long been acknowledged that *Fifty Shades of Grey* would be released as an R rated film. More dire stories instantly jumped to the notion that the all- important chemistry between Dakota and Jamie had ultimately not been that grand and that the reshoots were for the purpose of smoothing out some rough and awkward patches in the film.

Following the reshoots it was a time of relative relaxation for Dakota. The actress had just completed work on *A Bigger Splash* and was feeling fulfilled as a legitimate actress. Her personal life remained private although there had been, reportedly, the inevitable Italian guy in her life who she had made the acquaintance of while on location with *A Bigger Splash*. Which no less a personage than E.L. James had met briefly in London had gone on the internet to poo poo as a total rumor.

Dakota turned 25 not long after the *Fifty Shades* reshoots and, as befitting a wide-ranging circle of family and friends, she stretched the celebration out over a number of days. First off was a low key dinner with her father, followed by a casual spa day with her mother. But an informal hang out with close friends and several selfies was the one that got the most press interest thanks to one photo that featured Dakota's boyfriend Matt Hitt. It was the first photo of Hitt since the photo of Dakota and Matt being all warm and cozy in New York touched off the speculation and cemented the idea that they pair were truly a couple.

More information about the recent reshoots was slowly coming to light. And while the response remained mixed to the details, it definitely had shed further light on what had been going on.

Fifty Shades of Grey had become a cause celeb worldwide and, at a time when most pictures scheduled for a February 2015 release were already in the final stages of editing, the perfectionist approach of the producers and director were once again present. When it was deemed that a handful of scenes needed some tightening, Dakota and Jamie had been brought back to the *Fifty Shades* world for some additional reshoots in Vancouver. Dakota arrived in Vancouver relaxed and refreshed, confident that her post *Fifty* films were adding to the notion of her as a legitimate actress. Jamie, with his wife and child with him, was the picture of domestic bliss. But once director Young called action, they were immediately Anastasia and Christian once more.

The reshoots, including several scenes that established the kinky ground rules and an early passionate embrace and kiss, were, according to set reports, more natural and less mechanical the second time around. In between takes, Dakota and Jamie talked and laughed, catching up on all the events in their lives since the last time they had gotten together.

But nobody was prepared for the unexpected rush of bad press that surfaced immediately after the conclusion of the reshoots. *US Weekly* went big with the report that the reason for the reshoots was that Dakota, during a top secret test screening of the film, had come across as not very sensual and that the reshoots had been called for to up the actresses' on screen sex appeal. Universal Studios' publicity department was quick on the trigger to deny that Dakota's lack of sexual energy had been the reason for the reshoots.

But the bigwigs at the studio were also aware, whether they wanted to admit it or not, that the new wave of online film journalists could be a useful marketing tool as well as a harbinger of bad press. Some never had a bad thing to say about any project or celebrity in an attempt to curry favor and access. They were easy. Throw them all their press releases and the odd interview and they were happy. It was, however, the other end of the spectrum, the gossip mongers who could find something bad to say about anything, who could be a problem. And in the case of the reshoots and the doubts cast in Dakota's abilities, there was some concern.

Which was why, when they were contemplating the second trailer, set for a November release, it would be something that would focus on Dakota's sexuality as well as the chemistry between the actress and her hunky co-star. While the sense of romance was still there, much more time was added to the seduction and prolonged images of sexuality. The response to the second trailer was quite good but the question would only be answered when February rolled around and the fate of the film would be voted on by paying customers.

To add even more tension to Dakota's world, stories began circulating that the producers were planning on changing casts in the follow up films in the series. If Dakota was worried, she was not showing it.

But she would be quite pleased late in October when a bit of her cinematic past finally found a home. Despite good reviews and word of mouth, *Chloe and Theo* had been languishing in distribution hell and had barely been seen. That changed with the announcement that the film had been picked up for distribution by long-standing champion of independent films, Spotlight Pictures. One would assume that Dakota's sudden *Fifty Shades* notoriety would eventually spark interest in her lesser efforts and, to many observers, that seemed the case. But to Dakota and her fellow filmmakers, it did not matter what it took to finally give *Chloe and **Theo*** a chance.

CHAPTER NINETEEN
THE REST OF THE STORY

Dakota returned to New York following the *Fifty Shades* reshoots for some rest and relaxation. She used the opportunity to officially unveil the new man in her life, musician Matt Hitt, with what seemed, to the press, a pair of carefully choreographed appearances. The pair appeared up close and personal for the paparazzi at a book launch party for the book *Dressing For The Dark* and, a few days later, at opening night for the Broadway play *The Last Ship*. Throw in a fashion show appearance or two and some quality time with old friends and it was Dakota at her most relaxed, preparing for the public relations blitz for *Fifty Shades* that would, most certainly, see the actress up to her neck in interviews and around the world press junkets.

Her appearances with Matt were the only Dakota news of substance near year's end. The rest was largely nothing to fill in something in the news cycle. Such as the day a photo of Dakota taking her dog Zeppelin to the vet went viral. When the paparazzi caught Dakota and Matt eating yogurt it was a big deal. When Dakota and Melanie were spotted out shopping, the world that lived and died by celebrity scraps skipped a beat. The same could be said when a photo of Dakota exiting her gym had Dakota fanatics in a dither. The actress was also contributing to this run of non-news with playful Instagram photos of herself and her friends doing absolutely nothing.

In the meantime, Dakota seemed oblivious to the mania swirling around the upcoming *Fifty Shades of Grey* movie. If the paparazzi photos are any indication, Dakota was racking up frequent flyer miles between New York and Los Angeles during much of December, shopping sightseeing and doing nothing more ambitious than hanging out with friends.

But the actress could not help but have concerns, especially when the first trailer for the film was greeted with decidedly mixed reviews. In December the *Star* tabloid reported, with information courtesy of the ever-reliable 'unnamed source' that Dakota was, in fact, worried that the movie would turn out to be a worldwide joke ala that classic bomb *Showgirls.* Around the same time *TMZ* tracked down her mother, Melanie in Los Angeles and, once again got the always quotable actress to reiterate that she would not be seeing *Fifty Shades of Grey* because she did not think it was appropriate.

That this basic bit of old news would have any kind of traction the second time around was, by December, a fairly flimsy way of keeping Dakota's name in the public eye. And by comparison to her co-star Jamie, she needed it. Jamie continued to be busy post *Fifty Shades* and was always seemingly available for a quote. With all of Dakota's post *Fifty* films in the can and awaiting release, the actress really had little to do except occasionally drop some *Fifty Shades* hints that were, in this no man's land before the big press push, pretty much more of the same.

Without giving too much away, the public relations arm of the movie was more than happy to point out that the reshoots had gone splendidly and that the chemistry between the two stars was better than ever. But despite the happy talk emanating from publicists, the reality is that nobody would really know for sure until the film was actually seen. And it appeared that the film would not even remotely hit the screen until February 9, 2015 when a hip Hollywood cast and crew premiere would be held at an undisclosed location. The screening, complete with a glitzy after-party, would be a truly cathartic moment for all involved.

It was also announced that the prestigious Berlin Film Festival would be *Fifty Shades of Grey's* official international unveiling on February 11. Dakota sensed that while the Los Angeles showing would entail a high degree of drama and suspense as the first official showing of the film, Berlin, complete with red carpet appearances with Jamie, director Johnson and E.L. James, endless photo and interview sessions and the kind of traditional, old style Hollywood vibe, would ultimately be a lot more fun.

The gossip and tabloid press jumped on this news with an equally theatrical spin. Careers would be made or derailed based on what the audience saw on February 9th. Untold millions of dollars as well as professional reputations were at stake. It all sounded fairly outlandish to those outside the film community. But that tight-knit world, including Dakota, knew that, in a world where perception was nine points of show business law, it could all end up being true.

She was also secure in the notion that reviews, to a very large extent, would not matter. There would be some negative reviews for the sake of being controversial and contrary as well as the inevitable mixed reviews and the all-out raves which would be short on specifics and long on superlatives. But Dakota had the sense that *Fifty Shades of Grey* would be pretty much critic-proof and that it would be the vote of the people who were laying their money down that was finally the most important.

Dakota flew into Los Angeles on December 21st. After spending the previous weeks largely with her beau Hitt, she was now by herself but that would not be for long. It had been suggested by her parents that it would be nice if the whole family spent Christmas together. Dakota readily agreed, perhaps sensing that this might be the very last moments of normalcy in her life for some time to come.

Heading into the holiday season, Dakota seemed content and at peace with both her personal and professional life. She expressed as much in a late in the year interview with *Variety*. "I don't know if it [*Fifty Shades of Grey*] has changed my career yet but it is definitely different from all the roles I've taken. I'm a different person which each story that I've taken on."

In the same conversation Dakota inadvertently brought her career, from obscurity to being on the verge of stardom and all the personal and professional challenges she has dealt with, full circle. She had survived the past and the present and was now looking to the future.

As only somebody who had moved quite free and easy through the unnatural world of show business could.

"I grew up around talented people and it was the thing I loved the most. Acting is the place where I feel the most comfortable and I figured it was the thing I was supposed to do."

FILMOGRAPHY

A BIGGER SPLASH
(2015)
BLACK MASS
(2015)
FIFTY SHADES OF GREY
(2015)
CYMBELINE (AKA ANARCHY)
(2014)
NEED FOR SPEED
(2014)
DATE AND SWITCH (AKA GAY DUDE)
(2014)
CHOLE AND THEO
(2013)
THE FIVE YEAR ENGAGEMENT
(2012)
21 JUMP STREET
(2012)
GOATS
(2012)
FOR ELLEN
(2012)
BEASTLY
(2011)
THE SOCIAL NETWORK
(2010)
CRAZY IN ALABAMA
(1999)

TELEVISION

THE OFFICE
(2013)
BEN AND KATE
(2012)

SOURCES

I would like to thank Tom Todoroff and Tyler Shields for their cooperation and insights into little known aspects of Dakota Johnson's life and career.

NEWSPAPERS

The National Enquirer, The New York Post, The Hollywood Reporter, The New York Times Syndicate, The Los Angeles Times, Variety, Woman's Wear Daily, USA Today, Toledo Blade, The Independent, The Daily Mail, The Straits Times.

WEBSITES

Mail Online.com, The Wrap.com, Perez Hilton.com, Change.org, OMG Insider.com, IMDB.com, Starpulse.com, The Daily.com, Fashion United.com, The Maxx.com, Celebs.com, Zap2It.com, HitFlix.com, ShowbizSpy.com, Entertainmentwise. com, I'mNotObsessed.com, ENews.com, The National Ledger.com, Indiewire.com, up And Comers.com, Virgin Media.com

MAGAZINES

Entertainment Weekly, People, US, Aspen Peak, Interview, Details, Vanity Fair, Hello, American Profile, Teen Vogue, Elle, Cosmopolitan, AARP, California Lifestyle, The Last Magazine, Details, Vogue, Total Film, Watch.

MISCELLANEOUS

Matt Mueller (journalist), Ben and Kate (press junket), The Social Network (promo trailer), Beastly (production notes), The Sundance Film Festival (press junket), Funny Or Die (promo video), Elliot In The Morning (radio show), Need For Speed (promo trailer), Lorcano Film Festival (press conference).

TELEVISION

The Tom Snyder Show, Access Hollywood, The Jay Leno Show, The Graham Norton Show, The Today Show, Extra

For more books by Marc Shapiro visit
https://riverdaleavebooks.com/

The Secret Life of EL James: An Unauthorized
Biography
https://riverdaleavebooks.com/books/16/the-secret-life-
of-el-james

We Love Jenni: The Unauthorized Biography of Jenni
Rivera with Charlie Vazquez
https://riverdaleavebooks.com/books/28/we-love-jenni-
an-unauthorized-biography

Who Is Katie Holmes? An Unauthorized Biography
https://riverdaleavebooks.com/books/33/who-is-katie-
holmes-an-unauthorized-biography

Legally Bieber: Justin Bieber at 18
An Unauthorized Biography
http://riverdaleavebooks.com/books/41/legally-bieber-
justin-bieber-at-18

Annette Funicello: America's Sweetheart
An Unauthorized Biography
http://riverdaleavebooks.com/books/44/annette-
funicello-americas-sweetheart

Game: The Resurrection of Tim Tebow
An Unauthorized Biography
http://riverdaleavebooks.com/books/3084/game-the-
resurrection-of-tim-tebow

Lorde: Your Heroine
How This Young Feminist Broke the Rules and
Succeeded
http://riverdaleavebooks.com/books/4113/lorde-your-
heroine-how-this-young-feminist-broke-the-rules-and-
succeeded

ABOUT THE AUTHOR

Marc Shapiro is the *NY Times* best-selling author of *J.K. Rowling: The Wizard Behind Harry Potter*, *Justin Bieber: The Fever!* and many other best-selling celebrity biographies. He has been a free-lance entertainment journalist for more than twenty-five years, covering film, television, and music for a number of national and international newspapers and magazines. He has just finished *The Real Steele: The Unauthorized Biography of Dakota Johnson* and *Inside Grey's Anatomy: The Unauthorized Biography* of Jamie Dornan for Riverdaleavebooks.com.

Printed in Poland
by Amazon Fulfillment
Poland Sp. z o.o., Wrocław

33601509R00097